THE SALES INNOVATION PARADOX

"Over the past ten years, we have seen innovations in all aspects of buying and selling. Technology innovations allow sellers to do things that were impossible in the past. . . . All these innovations should enable us to drive step-function increases in revenue growth and value creation. But somehow we've failed. Percentage of reps making quota, average tenure in sales jobs, and employee engagement and satisfaction have plummeted. Customers are actively choosing rep-free buying experiences. . . .

It seems we have a paradox. Why are all these things that should be driving leaps in performance and value creation failing? Dr. Howard Dover gives us a perspective on the potential of these innovations, the challenges in harnessing their power, and some of what has driven failure. *The Sales Innovation Paradox* dives deeply into these issues, helping the reader understand both the potential and challenges. This book helps you rethink how you and your organizations might better harness the potential we have in driving sales and buying performance."

—DAVE BROCK, author of *Sales Manager Survival Guide* and CEO at Partners in EXCELLENCE

"Howard gets in the trenches with data, and in the celestial clouds, to paint a strategic horizon. The paradox that he talks about is not for the feeble; it's for the hungry, who want to skillfully create their future. The calm part of the book is the lull before he shoots you to the moon. It's best to mentally buckle up, 'cause when you hit zero gravity, and your mind is floating, you'll be looking at your future, with negative or positive g-force.

Anyone else frustrated with the black hole of innovation? Dover uses his PhD credential, love for data, calm demeanor, but incredibly biting desire to move people off their inertia pedestal and into action. If necessity is the mother of all invention, Dover is the godfather, offering perspective and a gentle (okay, all-out) push to move you to informed action regarding innovation in the firm and your career."

—ROBERT M. PETERSON, PhD, Dean's Distinguished Professor of Sales at Northern Illinois University

"If you're wondering why your return on the new sales enablement tool didn't materialize, you need to read this book. If you want to understand how to fix it, buy the book for your team."

—SCOTT GILLUM, founder and CEO of Carbon Design

"Paradoxes are intriguing, everywhere, and influential. When such seemingly counterintuitive propositions that relate to sales are not recognized and decoded, sales organizations are challenged and may decline. Howard Dover's *Sales Innovation Paradox* makes influential observations of the evolving world of sales and solves the sales innovation paradox to help us embrace new sales challenges with success. With the sales and technology adoption with behavior shifts (STABS) model, Dover enables the reader with a comprehensive understanding of the new strategic capabilities sales organizations and leaders need so that they can benefit from multiplier effects. *The Sales Innovation Paradox* is a beautiful tribute to the changing world of sales, where modern sales organizations need, more than ever, modern sales leaders."

—JOEL LE BON, PhD, professor of marketing and sales at Johns Hopkins University

"This sales book will define an era. Dr. Dover puts his finger right on the truth we've sensed is out there but now must urgently address. He gives us not only the well-research and reasoned background for the paradox but also tactical actions we can take to address it. Imagine the change that's possible if we made concern for the customer's reaction the center of our commercial strategy. It would be game-changing."

—SPENCER WIXOM, chief customer officer at Challenger

"Many companies have a lot of friction in their buying process. With the advent of more than a thousand sales apps, tools, and add-ons, there is often a classic sales process not leveraged by innovation. As Dr. Howard Dover shares, we need modern tools and modern motions. As long as our buyers are in a continual state of behavioral shift, our modern sellers will need to hone skills and also evolve. With all the change in the last few years, one message really stood out to me—that every company should question its existing revenue enablement structure (including talent) and realign to be more customer-centric."

—LORI RICHARDSON, sales strategist and author of *She Sells*

"This book should be rated D for disruption. Everything you've believed about sales will be called into question with this book. It disrupts norms, challenges your beliefs, and throws your core principles to the wind. But, unlike other books that leave you hanging, this one sets the table for the future of sales. This is the book that is the blueprint to follow."

—**MARK HUNTER**, author of *A Mind for Sales*

"Struggling to increase sales productivity? Find out why in *The Sales Innovation Paradox*. Better yet, discover how to achieve a sustainable multiplier effect, leading to true market dominance."

—**JILL KONRATH**, author of *Agile Selling* and *SNAP Selling*

"For years, sales organizations have fallen victim to the siren song of 'more'—hire more SDRs, buy more sales technology, complete more activities, implement more training, etc. Dr. Howard Dover uncovers the underappreciated sources of inertia holding us back from the promised land of increased sales efficiency and effectiveness. And it's not what you think. I recommend this book to any sales rep looking to become a modern-day sales professional."

—**JEN ALLEN**, chief evangelist at Challenger

"Howard eloquently shows us the past, present, and future of sales technology innovations. *The Sales Innovation Paradox* is a must-read for revenue leaders looking to accelerate successful and scalable go-to-market strategies, balancing technology with process and theory with practice. Reading this book will shine a light on ways to improve your sales efficiency and sales effectiveness."

—**ELAY COHEN**, cofounder of SalesHood
and author of *Enablement Mastery*

"If you have a sales team, you need to read this book. It not only gives you context and data on sales history; it gives you a road map and tools for how to shape your sales organization for the need of today and into the future. It's a must-read for all organizations wanting to grow and stay relevant with their customers."

—**JULIANA STANCAMPIANO**, author of *Radical Outcomes: How to Create Extraordinary Teams That Get Tangible Results*

"Dr. Dover provides us with an in-depth analysis of modern-day professional selling from three critical perspectives: the sellers, the buyers, and the sales leaders. He does an excellent job explaining the tools and technology available for salespeople, sales leaders, sales organizations, and the proper applications. He also provides an important perspective from the customer's point of view that will educate and reinforce the importance of proper preparation and sales motions by everyone who touches the customer. There is so much more on the pages that follow about resourcing, training, and the critical importance of the frontline sales leader. I thoroughly enjoyed this how-to guide to sales technology and would recommend it to salespeople, sales leaders, and sales executives regardless of industry."

—MIKE HART, former vice president of sales at Lennox

"*The Sales Innovation Paradox* highlights the unrivaled thirst of companies that try to adopt new and innovative technologies to improve their sales game but fall short of achieving their goals. Not all technologies are created equal, and few are grounded in the reality of the trench warfare salespeople need to go through to win the many battles required to close a deal. . . .

Dr. Howard Dover's advice is that of a seasoned sales practitioner and coach, guiding sellers on how to select the right technology and avoid becoming a victim of the sales innovation paradox. He guides us toward selecting technologies that are core to forging human relationships—the keystone of every major deal. Dr. Dover highlights how a fractured salestech landscape costs more to operate than the return on investment it promises to deliver. He also brings to the forefront the need to utilize the sales technology that is grounded in the practical reality of the heuristics of sales.

The Sales Innovation Paradox spoke to my heart (that of a sales and marketing futurist and innovator), as it highlights how technology needs to be developed to aid the needs of the people it serves and not the other way around. A must-read for anyone interested in lowering their cost of technology while improving their ROI."

—USMAN SHEIKH, founder and CEO of xiQ

THE SALES INNOVATION
PARADOX

HARNESSING MODERN METHODS FOR
OPTIMAL SALES PERFORMANCE

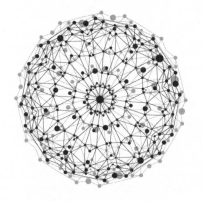

HOWARD DOVER, PhD

RIVER GROVE
BOOKS

Published by River Grove Books
Austin, TX
www.rivergrovebooks.com

Distributed by River Grove Books

Design and composition by Greenleaf Book Group and Mimi Bark
Cover design by Greenleaf Book Group and Mimi Bark
Cover image used under license from ©Shutterstock.com/13_Phunkod; ©Shutterstock.com/Quardia

Publisher's Cataloging-in-Publication data is available.

Print ISBN: 9781632996244

eBook ISBN: 9781632996251

First Edition

To my wife and best friend, Amy. Thanks for all the adventures we have had in life and for being my best coach and advocate in all that I do.

CONTENTS

FOREWORD

When we consider the incredible amount of sales technology introduced over the last five years, we can't help but believe we're living
in a golden age of selling. After all, we're now equipped to get more
done in less time, at greater scale, with higher accuracy, than ever before.
Indeed, the potential for increased productivity from recent sales innovation seems nearly boundless.

Yet sometimes when I think about how all that new technology is
actually affecting day-to-day sales activity—particularly from a *customer's*
perspective—it leaves me wondering whether we're living in a golden age
of selling at all, or if we're perhaps instead starring in the final scene of the
1968 classic *Planet of the Apes.* Somehow, it seems, we blew it all up. It
makes you wonder: How could we have gone so wrong?

But here we are.

This is the sales innovation paradox—in which increasingly powerful sales technology renders professional sellers increasingly better at
making buying experiences significantly worse.

How exactly? Part of the problem lies in the fact that a great deal
of sales innovation isn't designed to *improve* sales behavior so much
as to *scale* it, through automation, integration, and simplification.
Ironically, this technological bias toward efficiency means that bad

behavior becomes *amplified* rather than rectified. After all, there's an almost unavoidable human belief that if a little bit of something is a good thing, then a whole lot of the same thing must be a great thing. So whatever we're going to do with technology, let's be sure to do it *a lot*.

As a result, many sellers lean into technology to do exactly that: more. To send out more emails, voicemails, InMails, and video messages through more channels to more people than ever before—the same people who are already inundated with unrelenting, unwanted, and unhelpful outreach from other sales reps employing the exact same strategy.

It's become so bad, in fact, that most of us no longer answer our phones. Few of us engage with unsolicited emails. And many of us complain loudly about endless amounts of poorly targeted, highly scripted, impersonal sales outreach through social media.

Yet, ironically, when companies find their technology-fueled customer engagement strategies falling short, the natural inclination isn't to reconsider or to pull back but to double down, possibly even hiring more reps to do exactly the same thing. After all, the best way to overcome weak results is with increased volume.

The implications of this for the broader sales profession are potentially profound and possibly even existential.

A bit too dramatic? Maybe not. In fact, we can see clear signs of sales's waning relevance in well-publicized B2B (business-to-business) buying research from leading advisory firms like Gartner. In a recent Gartner study, more than 43 percent of B2B buyers—and 54 percent of millennials—reported a clear preference for buying even the most complex solutions without speaking to a sales rep at all.[1] Even more dramatically, Gartner reports that number to have increased to more than 70 percent in just the last year.[2]

Bottom line: B2B buyers increasingly prefer a rep-free experience. And one can't help but conclude that that sentiment is tied directly to customers' rapidly diminishing belief that sales rep interactions provide any substantive value. After all, if the role of today's sales rep is to use new and improved technologies to spam me in highly performative but otherwise meaningless scripted communications again and again through every imaginable communications channel, including my personal cell phone, then the only real need I have for a sales rep is the need for them to go away and leave me alone.

This is *not* where sales innovation was supposed to take us.

And the frustrating thing is that we've done this to ourselves. At scale. With technology.

So which is it? The golden age of selling or the final death throes of a widely reviled sales profession falling into increasing irrelevance? And how could technology specifically designed to make things so much better have led to a place where things have become so much worse?

Enter Howard Dover to help us unravel this mystery, taking us step-by-step through the sales innovation paradox—where it came from, why it persists, and most importantly, what to do about it.

So how do we realize the good of innovation without falling victim to the siren song of mediocrity at scale? Well, the answer can't be to retreat from sales innovation altogether, especially at a time when both the pace and the quality of the innovation are constantly increasing. As Howard demonstrates, there are indeed massive benefits associated with new sales technology, making it unwise to eschew its continued adoption. The problem isn't adoption; it's application. Howard makes a strong case for a far more principled approach to the use of technology—one based less on helping sellers sell and far more on *helping buyers buy.*

The proper sales "motions," he argues, will be highly contextual, based on the specific needs of a customer buying group at a particular point in their buying journey given the specific buying "job" they're seeking to complete at that time.

What does this world of customer-centric sales motions look like exactly, and how can technology help? Read on, for the answers are not only compelling but critically important to our very survival as a relevant profession.

Enjoy the read.

Brent Adamson
Author of *The Challenger Sale*

PREFACE

I started in sales at a young age, when I needed money for camping gear in my early teens. I had a sales company to put myself and my wife through college and to start our young family. During this time, I was struck one day by a book review for *Strategic Database Marketing* by Arthur Hughes.[1] After consuming the book, I started my journey as a data scientist and technologist. I applied database technology to that business and found efficiency gains, greater sales, and less turnover. I was hooked!

For about five years, I worked for the government and automated business processes with technology. I witnessed firsthand the power of technology to create greater data accuracy and reduce tedious manual processes, which allowed many professionals to spend more time analyzing results rather than developing a report.

I have advocated the use of technology in professional sales and business-to-business marketing. I have taken the stage at national events to discuss the automation of our field and the augmentation of our salespeople. But along the way, I started to see something that didn't make sense to me. While some companies were experiencing the productivity gains that I had always witnessed in my career, many sales organizations were not seeing productivity gains from technology adoption and implementation.

This didn't make sense to me. Early on, I saw this as more of an adoption problem, meaning that companies were not moving fast enough to adopt new innovations. But as more and more companies spent significant amounts on sales technology, I witnessed the reverse of what I had seen in my earlier professional career. Both independent companies and the entire field were not only failing to experience productivity gains but also adding more headcount and achieving less. What happened to the experience curve[2] and the productivity gains that should result from such investments?

I have been on a journey for several years to explore this paradox, which I call the sales innovation paradox. The bad news is that the issues seem pervasive. The good news is that some companies have cracked the paradox and are experiencing the exponential gains we would have expected.

Although I am an academic by trade, I am a sales technologist at heart. In this book, I seek to address executive leadership and the sales profession, not my academic colleagues. I hope that I hit that mark. I hope these thoughts start a conversation and that we can experience the progress that will allow the professional sales field to better support their goals with the work they do every day.

INTRODUCTION

We have witnessed a historic and tectonic shift in the business-to-business sales field over the past few years. This shift is partially due to the exponential increase in technology applications and software available to assist efficiency and effectiveness. At the same time, sales enablement has gone from a marginal concept to the point where most firms—over 60 percent—invest in it[1] and over 85 percent report having a function dedicated to it.[2] Furthermore, we are spending between $15 billion and $20 billion a year on sales training.[3] With such substantial investments in sales, we should be witnessing a corresponding increase in sales productivity. However, we have been experiencing a decrease in quota attainment for several years.[4] Some would say that quotas are being set too high. Perhaps, but we also increased the number of people in sales development representative (SDR) roles by over 570 percent from 2012 to 2018,[5] and an additional 86 percent from 2018 to 2021.[6] We have innovated, trained, enabled, and expanded our sales function, yet performance is at a historic low! This is the sales innovation paradox: Although we embrace all the available improvements, our results stagnate. It needs to be diagnosed and treated so that our field can reach new levels of efficiency and effectiveness. Sales is a great profession that needs great leaders and great minds to move our field into the next era of sales.

The current phenomenon is understandable. Companies have spent more on training to help our salespeople become better at their trade, but the sales force continues to miss their quotas. The reduction in performance per salesperson[7] has caused sales leadership and management to invest in technology and sales operations, but this has not fixed the problem. Where sales operations, training, and technology have failed, the contemporary solution is to invest in sales enablement. Finally, when quota attainment continued to drop and all other attempts failed, many firms adjusted and increased their sales force. We have witnessed a transition from field sales to inside sales in the past decade.[8] A reorganization of sales development has created new roles, including lead development representatives (LDR) and SDRs.[9] In addition, many are following the strategy used by Salesforce to get to the first $100 million.[10] If we were tracking a Gartner hype cycle,[11] we might consider the field in the trough of disillusionment, because we are just learning how to operate with all this innovation. The sales field is consuming innovation at a rapid pace, but the early results are not encouraging.

Our friends at Gartner indicate that technology innovation often follows a hype cycle.[12] When innovation is created or discovered, we are excited about its potential, and we may hit a peak of inflated expectations. Following this peak, we no longer buy all the buzz, and we enter the trough of disillusionment. This moment is a critical inflection point as the innovation dies off as just a fad or begins to be understood sufficiently to make an impact in the field along the slope of enlightenment. During this period, we can see the gains of efficiency play out till we reach the actual plateau of productivity.

Investment in technology and process innovation usually leads to higher performance and efficiency. The concept of the experience curve indicates that firms learn as they produce.[13] This learning should lead to efficiency over time. Moore's law describes continually increasing efficiency in the field of computing.[14] The law states that the capacity of computer chips will double about every two years, while the cost of producing those chips will be cut in half. While sales is clearly different from computing, we have seen nothing similar to the experience curve despite substantial investments in technology. In fact, as a field, the data indicates decay in efficacy. While the sales field continues to innovate, the typical efficiency from learning has yet to materialize.

The purpose of this book is to break down the potential causes of the sales innovation paradox. Specifically, I aim to answer the following questions:

- What is the status of sales today?

- Where should we be if sales followed the experience curve, given the existing investment and innovation in training, sales methodologies, and sales technologies?

- What is stopping us from getting to higher performance levels?

- Are we nearing the tipping point where leadership, investors, and owners will alter their funding of the sales machine as we know it?

- Who is disrupting this paradox, what are they doing, and how are they achieving these outcomes?

As long as sales organizations focus internally, the sales innovation paradox will continue. Unlike most other functions of the firm, where internal focus leads to efficiency gains, the process of generating revenue via sales is highly dependent on several external factors—most importantly, the customer. It is essential to understand the buyer's location on their customer journey and to realize this is not a static question. I propose that the customer is in a continuous state of behavioral shift. In this book, I dissect the different elements and dynamic nature of the customer's behavioral shift. I discuss critical cycles that provide insights necessary to diagnose what may be impeding our progress toward efficiency gains. Furthermore, I explore how technological innovation leads to a multifaceted behavioral shift by both customers and companies.

After diagnosing the sales innovation paradox, I explore how individuals, teams, and even organizations can break the cycle. I present sales productivity data gathered on more than 1,000 companies to identify which ones are breaking from the paradox. Using examples from companies and individuals, we can see how they move from stagnancy to multiplier effects. It starts with a strategy to make the customer the design point and to understand the nature of the customer behavioral shift. If your company's sales are suffering from the paradox, your organization will need to develop strategies to remove or mitigate the structural forces that create and sustain its inertia. As you make your customers' needs and behavior the core design point of your go-to-market strategy, you will see the efficiency and effectiveness that will escape without this focus.

Once these principles are understood, we will see exponential increases in sales effectiveness. Revenue generation will become efficient and predictable. I identify and analyze examples of individuals, teams, and organizations who have experienced this multiplier effect. They have experienced productivity gains of up to 1,000 percent in the early stages of deployment.

We are clearly in an era where we can mechanize, automate, and augment the capacity of our sales organizations. The investment in and deployment of technology in our field has led to an expanded capacity to deliver customer messages. However, we are experiencing a unique moment as more and more companies deploy technology without considering the ecological cost to the market that brings them revenue. As the business-to-business market scales up automation and mechanized capacity, we would do well to contemplate what effect all this has on our customers.

A few years ago, at the inaugural Sales Enablement Society meeting in Dallas, Texas, I was asked to set the stage for the event and to discuss where the field is headed. As I prepared for that moment, I realized the similarity between our current time and that of the Dust Bowl of the 1930s. In the early twentieth century, mechanization allowed farmers to plow vast areas of ground with new disc plows. This change allowed farmers to plow up more than 30 rows at one time. At first, there was a substantial increase in the amount of wheat harvested. Of course, this eventually led to a drop in the prices, which led some farmers in Texas, Arizona, Oklahoma, and Colorado to do a fall bumper crop. However, what they didn't know at the time was that their technique was causing soil erosion. As the drought came, the shallow topsoil simply flew away and created the most significant ecological disaster in US agricultural history.

The analogy is timely. We have just developed and deployed the ability to mechanize the message delivery of our sales machine. Not only have we automated our field and augmented our salespeople, but we have also increased the number of people we use to do this. This sounds like a bumper crop strategy, doesn't it? But the harvest from our efforts is decaying, just like the failed wheat yield that led to the Dust Bowl. We have plowed the field with 30 disc plows but failed to recognize the impact on the customer (the soil), and we are experiencing a critical moment in our industry.

Those organizations, sales leaders, and sales contributors who recognize the trend and start adjusting their strategy will find huge returns. In contrast, those who continue along the current path will find themselves sitting in a sales Dust Bowl. It is not sufficient to identify a best practice, scale it, and reap a harvest in the modern world of sales machine mechanization and amplification. You are working in near Dust Bowl conditions in many markets, and you only have so much control over the environment you work in. But those who pivot, shift their behavior, and then enhance the modern seller with modern motions, automation, and augmentation will find cost reductions and sales force productivity gains that have evaded them in the past.

As we consider the success of the FAANGM group (Facebook, Apple, Amazon, Netflix, Google, and Microsoft), we begin to discover that the customer has substantially changed and continues to change as they adopt and engage with technology. These consumers are your buyers; they are not just dormant soil or a static object. These consumers make up the buying teams that create a dynamic market resulting from various waves of innovation, adoption, and related behavioral shifts. Scaling the old sales machine to address this market has led to the sales innovation paradox. But if you understand this new reality and change the way you go to market, your company will be able to outperform the competition. We have entered the next era of selling. Are you ready?

CHAPTER 1

THE SALES TECH EXPLOSION

In 1994, Blockbuster video was at its peak with over 9,000 locations. They were dominating their market. By 2019, over 9,000 retail locations closed,[1] and there is only one remaining Blockbuster location, in Bend, Oregon. Countless news sources have documented the continuing demise of the retail sector that started well before the COVID-19 global pandemic. This disruption and transformation haven't just affected the consumer market; they have also affected the business-to-business market. The new video streaming leader is now Netflix, and the new dominant player in e-commerce is Amazon. Netflix and Amazon join the other digital transformation winners often referred to as the FAANG stocks—Facebook, Amazon, Apple, Netflix, and Google. We would be remiss if we did not add M to this list (FAANGM) to include Microsoft.

Amazon, which started as an online book reseller, has grown into a digital distribution phenomenon, spanning online shopping, entertainment distribution, and cloud infrastructure. This transition from brick-and-mortar retail to online has created a traditional-retail graveyard with brands like Sears, Kmart, Toys "R" Us, RadioShack, Circuit City, and others having declared bankruptcy or restructured. These trends have only been accelerated by the global pandemic, with e-commerce doing ten years of growth in under one year.[2] We have indeed moved from going to the mall to expecting front-door delivery in two days or less.

Apple and other competitors in the mobile space have transformed our mobile phone experience. Apple iTunes changed the music industry by allowing customers to purchase single songs as digital downloads. They developed a generation of people who are willing to pay for digital music, and mobile device users became accustomed to buying digital goods (such as music) via their phones and through digital marketplaces. This behavioral change led to the acceptance of and demand for various digital goods.[3] Apple opened up a digital marketplace for games, music, books, apps, and more. These developments, along with advances in the technology itself, transitioned our mobile phones from making phone calls to being a supercomputer in the palm of our hands—and a powerful, ubiquitous purchasing tool.

Netflix started as a simple concept: a monthly subscription to watch a few videos each month. You would order DVDs from your computer, and they would arrive by mail. This innovation was to combat late fees at video stores such as the once-mighty Blockbuster Video chain. With the advent of video streaming, Netflix was able to simplify its content delivery model to stream video content directly to your computer and, eventually, to your mobile device. Move forward to today's world of anywhere-anytime video streaming services, and Netflix has forever altered the entertainment delivery model. Now, anyone can watch just about any entertainment content from any location on any device for a low monthly fee. This model has become so disruptive that major entertainment companies such as Disney, Comcast, and others have developed their own services. Meanwhile, broadcast TV and cable services have been suffering from the changes as customers are free to choose where and how to purchase and consume entertainment.[4]

Google started as a simple concept to help make the internet navigable. Although it wasn't the first search engine, it was arguably the most powerful and definitely the most successful. Flash forward to today, and Google dominates the search category. While other companies and concepts have tried, only Baidu in China and Yangtze in Russia have cracked Google's global dominance in search. Almost every company that exists must have a Google strategy. Google's existence has given us the concept of search engine optimization and tools like Google AdWords and Google Analytics. Google also became the dominant player in video with their acquisition of YouTube in 2006, and they have a presence in the mobile arena, the social space, and the IoT (Internet of Things). Google's new Home apps allow us to automate our homes, get answers to our questions, and shop online with voice commands, competing with Amazon's Alexa.

Facebook and other social media companies have manifested a social transformation in our society. The world now connects via groups and friends on social platforms. The world gets its information from its social network faster than traditional forms of knowledge like TV, radio, and newspapers. Facebook has remained dominant in this space by purchasing Instagram[5] and WhatsApp.[6] Facebook has also become another source of advertising, further diluting the ad dollars spent by advertisers on traditional forms of media.[7]

So how has this digital shift affected business-to-business buyers and sellers? While the marketing technology explosion has received much attention over the years, with just under 10,000 applications, according to Scott Brinker, the sales technology explosion has just begun.[8] Nancy Nardin and Nicolas De Kouchkovsky maintain documentation of separate sales technology landscapes, showing over 1,000 and 1,100 technologies, respectively.[9]

Several new companies provide a means to select which sales technology to choose for a sales organization. Vendor Neutral is developing assessment tools to assist companies' sales technology strategies.[10] G2 Crowd has also begun providing sales technology coverage on many categories from the sales tech landscape and is designed to provide a service similar to Yelp's consumer review resource.[11] Gartner provides coverage in the larger areas of complete business process applications, such as customer relationship management (CRM) software. These applications go from point solutions (applications that automate or augment a specific function in the sales process or customer journey) to complete sales cycle solutions. These apps are intended to automate and augment the seller's job to multiply our existing sales and marketing efforts and motions.

SOCIAL SELLING

According to CSO Insights, most sales organizations have initiated social selling initiatives in the past few years.[12] The concept of social selling still brings confusion to both sales and marketing organizations alike. While social marketing is well understood, the idea of social selling is still relatively new. Therefore, some may struggle to define its meaning, let alone execute a social selling strategy. But we must be clear that social selling is not social marketing.

The advent of social media has opened up a new channel to communicate with and influence our customers. While the concept and strategy of social selling have diffused across most business-to-business sellers, the depth of design and efficacy is still in its early phases. According to LinkedIn's "State of Sales, 2018" report, 59 percent of companies say they use social selling.[13] Despite this majority adoption, there are still sufficient areas to debate social selling's impacts on actual sales effectiveness and efficiency.

There are very few resources available and limited rigorous research on what is effective in social selling. We are currently operating with mostly successful case studies but lack the large-scale scientific research studies to explore social selling's effectiveness. It is clear that social is a place where consumers and organizational buyers spend time gathering information and communicating. Therefore, social is another channel to provide content and direct communication with our target audience for the business-to-business market.

BEHAVIORAL TRACKING

What if we could target the ideal customer—the customer who is searching for our product? It would be ideal to target the customer who has purchased a complimentary product or service, meaning a product that often leads to a purchase of your product. What if we could target the customer based on trigger events, like online downloads of a competitor's white papers in the business sector or when someone's activity hints at a life event like a marriage, a birth, or a move to a new city?

For quite some time, digital cookies have been able to track the actions of users as they move from site to site on the web. The *Wall Street Journal* series "What They Know" has documented how extensive behavioral tracking has become.[14] Companies can track and sell access to a consumer's browsing history and their movements and actions on their mobile phone because many users allow location and other tracking services when they download free mobile applications. We live in a world where complex algorithms and machines allow us to predict purchase behaviors in the consumer market with a remarkably high degree of accuracy.

Since all business-to-business buyers and influencers are also consumers, these data points are also available for the business sector, not just the consumer sector. We can add consumer tracking and customer and company data to predict where a customer is in their buyer's journey. More targeted business market nurturing campaigns and outreach strategies can help develop greater campaign efficacy and sales force deployment. Data providers such as ZoomInfo provide purchase intent data as part of their service.

SALES ENABLEMENT

Sales enablement originated in the technology sector around 2007 from research analysts.[15] The basic concept was that marketing struggled to provide training and content valued by the sales organization and their customers, so a new role was developed that would take the product and messaging from marketing and prepare it for the sales organization to use via training, onboarding, and content development.

The concept of sales enablement remained relatively unknown to the greater business sales community until about 2016 or 2017. However, starting in 2017, we experienced exponential growth in the number of people given the title. This exponential growth in the sales enablement role also expanded the support request from sales enablement professionals.[16] Moving beyond a role between marketing and sales, it morphed into a position that assists with overall sales force efficiency and effectiveness, not just content and training for new products and markets. More and more companies are allocating more significant headcount and resources to this function, and the concept of sales enablement is no longer straightforward to define. Robert Peterson and I have written an academic paper that categorized the dirty dozen definitions of this field.[17]

EXPONENTIAL SALES PERFORMANCE

One thing is clear: We have never had more resources available to the sales community. We have been training our salespeople in social selling, as well as aligning our marketing and sales functions. We can use technology to track the movement of our buyers and customers in both the consumer and business markets. We continue to add technology to assist the customer and the sales organization to allow revenue to come into our firm with less friction than ever before. So the need for a modern adjustment to our go-to-market strategies has never been greater.

We can serve the customer with content relevant to their customer journey with automated processes and augmented salespeople.

So our capacity to experience exponential sales performance has never been greater. We should reach existing markets with lower headcount, enter markets that were not cost-effective before, and dominate markets at a speed that we have not been able to in the past. But are we experiencing these benefits from our investments? That is the central question I seek to explore in this book. I attempt to identify the root cause of the sales innovation paradox and then seek those outliers in the market who have overcome these issues and have moved on to the next era of selling in the modern economy.

What Can We Learn?

- Consumers have been affected by the consumer technology sector, with companies like Facebook, Google, and Netflix changing go-to-market strategies.

- Sales organizations have experienced social selling, the sales technology explosion, and behavioral tracking, which provide new opportunities for business-to-business sales organizations.

- Sales organizations have an opportunity for exponential gains with appropriate strategy and go-to-market models.

CHAPTER 2

THE POTENTIAL OF INNOVATION

The sales field has experienced an accelerated pace of technology innovation over the past few years. However, it is crucial to recognize that the various players in the market adopt and adapt these innovations differently. Technology has opened opportunities for salespeople, sales managers, and organizations. If companies and sales teams could harness all the innovation developed over the past few years, what could their success look like?

We should see gains in both efficiency and effectiveness from our sales organizations. These combined effects should lead to higher profits driven by a lower cost of sales and greater revenue from customers who have excellent and seamless experiences.

THE SALES PERSPECTIVE

Sales firms are currently struggling with technology adoption, including the most basic sales technology of CRM. From a sales perspective, the fundamental problem with CRM is that the systems rarely provide sufficient value for the salesperson entering the data. The secondary problem is the very fact that salespeople are required to enter the data. Taking the time to document calls, emails, LinkedIn communications, face-to-face meetings, and so on is very time consuming.

To get a feel for where we could be, let's look over at the consumer side. With the digitization of the consumer sector, firms capture data electronically via observation (web clicks) and purchase history (online ordering and/or loyalty card programs). As the consumer side of the business has moved to ubiquitous data capture, the amount of data on customer interaction has exploded, and the field has innovated accordingly.

Since the business-to-business side relies on documentation from sales, salespeople do not get the same level of data capture and customer journey transparency as the consumer side. As long as data capture in the sales field requires manual input, we will struggle to innovate. The recent sales tech category of sales engagement introduces technology capable of capturing critical data from observation rather than from manual data entry. Companies like Outreach, Salesloft, and VanillaSoft work to capture motions and engagement. These tools provide battle cards and templates to use through the sales process, while, behind the scenes, they capture the engagement data without the sales force needing to separately document their activities. These platforms provide both tools for the salesperson and data collection for the company, allowing a more holistic view of the customer.

To allow for a more consistent customer engagement process, nurturing campaigns or sequences encourage those customers who are not ready to buy. While salespeople will remain important in those purchases, where the customer prefers or requires human interaction, some of these tasks are simply hard for one person to remember and to have time to complete. We can use automation to perform some of the redundant tasks performed by salespeople when the primary customer data and the related touchpoints are documented more accurately in the single source of customer data. Sales engagement software enables follow-up communication at scheduled intervals, meeting reminders, profile data from LinkedIn and other sources before a meeting, and many other tasks. Likewise, new technologies can read emails and meeting transcripts provided by voice-to-text tools; this automation can capture tasks that the salesperson may overlook or forget. As we capture more data in ways that augment the sales motion rather than slow it down, we will see more appropriate and timely sales efforts, leading to more frequent and valuable customer engagement in the sales process.

Although technology can automate redundant sales functions, the more significant impact will be when technology augments our sales organizations. We will see intelligence aggregated into a comprehensive user interface showing insights from LinkedIn, Twitter, and news feeds. AI and back-end sales support will be queuing up movements within the buying team. Job changes and social media activity will provide just-in-time buying team insights to allow sellers to better see key buying queues in the buying process. Currently, technology tracks sales or marketing-generated emails as they make their way through the customer organization. Sales engagement tools provide valuable information on who has opened the email, who has shared the email, how long they spent on the email, and so on. Soon, we can expect to see buying bots doing the preliminary fact gathering for customers, leading us to the moment where bots are engaging bots to gather and develop information on both sides of the buying and selling process.[1]

The increase in available data can allow our internal systems to analyze internal touchpoint data and competitor data from third-party behavioral observations to provide a buying journey picture across multiple buyers on the buying team. Gartner's research shows that only 17 percent of the buyer process involves talking with a sales representative.[2] As customers turn to more and more digital sources, we will see enhanced abilities to track those journeys to allow sales teams to spend time with the right customers in the funnel, to achieve their potential efficiency gains.

When you combine voice-to-text, the ability to analyze the tone and context of calls, and personality data, we can see how deal-coaching and determining the best approach to each buyer can be augmented now and may soon become automated and ubiquitous. These capabilities are already in beta testing at some technology companies.

The sales tools are also available to allow organizations to enhance sales organization performance. With the advent of AI tools, we should experience accelerated learning and skill development to decrease onboarding times. These advances are possible via enhanced training methods that can span beyond just onboarding into overall training and skill development. With conversation intelligence and sales engagement tools, we can observe and analyze the selling motions of our team and assess their effectiveness in various and changing buyer situations. Sales leadership, management, and support will have greater visibility and intelligence regarding the current skills and competency of the sales organization at the salesperson level, with relevant and timely detailed insights. This intelligence should lead to enhanced coaching opportunities.

Salespeople receive coaching, but tools can also analyze the coaching sessions to develop managers and support staff with better coaching skills. This level of analysis and execution would help build more profound leadership within our sales organizations.

Cost Advantages

If we can harness performance differences, our acquisition and revenue costs would naturally decrease. With performance improved by 10–50 times, I can accomplish 10–50 times the revenue with the same sales headcount.[3] Although this outcome requires other investments in technology, support, training, and enablement, it is improbable that the additional costs would reduce the overall efficiency gains. These cost advantages will allow your company to increase the compensation for top talent, address more market segments, increase the velocity of go-to-market strategies, and allow new business models to develop.

But not all companies have or will transition to modern motions and methods. Some will adopt a few innovations, but only if you strategically deploy all modern motions will you experience the full multiplier effect. Let's first discuss the talent and market segment advantages and then talk about go-to-market strategies and business models.

TALENT AND SEGMENTS

To state the obvious, if you can multiply your sales force productivity by 10–50 times, you are producing what 10–50 salespeople accomplished previously with one person. Let's consider two different companies. One uses modern motions and has experienced a tenfold gain in productivity; the control company has not adopted any new motions or methods. From the start, we assume that Modern, Inc., produces 10 times the revenue of Classic Sales Machine, Inc. (CSMI). Let's assume that the two companies make a similar product and compete directly in the same market for the same customers. CSMI produces $250,000 in revenue per salesperson, and Modern, Inc., has $2.5 million in revenue per salesperson. For the sake of argument, we will assume a 50 percent margin, not including sales commissions.

With a 50 percent margin, CSMI has $125,000 per salesperson for commission sharing, while Modern, Inc., has 1.25 million. Modern, Inc., could compensate their salespeople at twice the rate of CSMI, but let's assume that they only pay 1.5 times CSMI's rate. Taking all else as equal, Modern, Inc., will be able to hire away the best talent in the industry. If you are hiring the best sales talent, you will get even more revenue. Those salespeople will also experience more success. With a clear advantage, Modern, Inc., will win the talent war and will more easily retain their sales team.

With a reduced cost of acquisition, Modern, Inc., can also afford to do two very strategic moves. First, they can address new markets that were not cost efficient before. If your cost to acquire is 10 percent of what it used to be, unprofitable segments are now profitable. Second, with a lower cost structure, the overall price of the product or service can be made more competitive. Modern, Inc., gains a competitive advantage over CSMI at a lower price point, which opens up additional market segments. This upward spiral of advantages can lead to market dominance.

TO-MARKET VELOCITY

If one salesperson can perform at tenfold efficiency, I can cover my market 10 times faster. For new products, services, and start-ups, we can fail fast or win fast. What might have taken 18–24 months to determine in the past now takes only a month or two. All of a sudden, getting the messaging and targeting right seems essential. When you think about the implication of these statements, you will begin to see why organizations, executives, and managers may feel a degree of anxiety about modern concepts.

But if productivity can be multiplied by 10 or 50, those who embrace modern methods can develop market dominance. Let's assume an addressable market of 10,000 customers between CSMI and Modern, Inc. If we assume 10 customers per month with a classic strategy per headcount and if we hire 100 salespeople, we can get to the 10,000 customer coverage in 10 months. However, we must hire, train, and retain 100 salespeople, and only half of them will obtain a quota. We will lose 20–40 percent of our sales team each year. We assume a six-month onboarding process, hiring 10 sales managers and only hiring 10–20 salespeople per month. Let's compare the two companies. We assume 10 hires per month, six months to full productivity (with 15 percent of full production gained each month until fully trained), and 30 percent turnover every six months due to exit or promotion (we have to get managers from somewhere).

Modern, Inc., would need to hire 10 salespeople. Since they are paying 1.5 times the market average, they will be able to attract top talent from existing firms and in the entry-level market. Assuming they can only hire 10 people per month, they will have their whole team ready in six months. By six months, Modern, Inc., will achieve 14 percent of the market to CSMI's 5.8 percent. At the end of the year, we have 66.5 percent for Modern and 34.7 percent for CSMI (see appendix B for a detailed analysis). At this point, CSMI has five cohorts still onboarding when the market becomes addressed. While this is just an exercise, it should give you pause to consider these points. Market dominance is possible quite quickly. We haven't even added the effect of automation in this example; this use of automation and the market dominance concept lead us to consider new business models.

NEW BUSINESS MODELS

We can see that market testing and market dominance are possible via modern methods, automation, or both. We see more and more companies choosing to follow the software as a service (SaaS) go-to-market model. They decide to hire SDRs and use tools to address the market with high velocity. My own research reveals that, over the past few years, this trend has amplified, with sales development becoming 65 percent of all sales positions, versus 50 percent in 2018 (see figure 2.1).

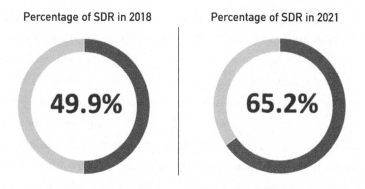

Figure 2.1. Sales development representative growth, 2018–2021.

Given the challenge with ramping up for new products, we will begin to see more channel partners and other hybrid models that will allow a third party to become Modern, Inc. When channel partners exist with modern salespeople in place, they can condense the onboarding cycle and product training to accelerate market launch and market share capture. These trends will be especially true for companies residing in the CSMI mode.

Sales versus Digital

Because customers obtain more and more of their information from digital channels and social networks, as your company invests more funds into the digital side of the business, you will see more significant sales gains for a lower cost. These gains will allow you to move down-market and service more mid-market and small and medium businesses that were previously unreachable with traditional sales structures because of high costs and low profit. However, as you realize these efficiencies, your company will digitize more and more revenue upmarket. Identifying which transactions, segments, and markets should be simply digitally captured with limited to no salesperson coverage will lead to higher profit margins and more agility to move with customer behavior. If you properly transform your revenue-generating model, your company will develop a competitive advantage in its speed to market, cost, and customer experience.

These changes will most likely require your company to question your existing structures and realign to be more customer-centric. You might question the role of sales or of marketing. You might wonder what various titles really mean—sales enablement, sales operations, sales effectiveness, even customer service and success. You might question your incentive systems, given the new revenue generation motions and customer expectations. Likely, you will not find your current silo-based organizational structures to be the highly effective agile strategy the modern buyer expects.

For those companies that can't make this transition fast enough, we will see a greater degree of outsourcing and channel growth. These firms will find it more efficient and effective to outsource marketing and even sales functions when their internal organization cannot develop agility. We will see that firms that specialize in certain sales motions are better able to adjust to the buyer behavioral changes in the market. The extreme of this strategy is that your channel partners may prove more agile in their market movements, so more companies will need to use agile channel partners as a counterstrategy to their internal inability to adjust. Firms that focus on moving trends and technology will be better situated to generate revenue in many circumstances and markets. We see this with the growth of companies such as SHI International, Ring Central, and other third-party resellers in the tech space.

Constraining Factors

There are two types of sales professionals: those who see potential in modern methods and those who deny or fear their existence. Is it any wonder that 85–90 percent of professionals in the field are building, are working for, or were created by the CSMIs of the world? Any individual, manager, enablement professional, or executive who wants to deploy modern concepts will face significant internal and external inertia, because most of the sales field only has experience working for CSMI. A vast majority of the sales field, by definition, is and will be stuck in a company with an outdated sales machine.

Beware of the Modern-Day Suitcase Farmer

Before the Dust Bowl era, anyone could claim their plot of land in Oklahoma. If you showed up at the county courthouse and registered, you received a plot of land. While this government allocation of land was intended to populate the state of Oklahoma, it gave rise to the suitcase farmer, a businessperson from the eastern United States who would travel by train to Oklahoma, claim their land, pay a farmer in the area to till and plant their land, and come back with a suitcase to collect their payment from the harvest. The arrival of suitcase farmers only exacerbated the number of acres plowed with poor farming techniques. These poor techniques were the root cause of the Dust Bowl.

Suitcase farmers arrived because of the incentives in the market. Anyone could claim the land and farm it. There was no enforced requirement that the owner of the land would live there. The costs to plow and plant the land versus the returns from the harvest were a good investment, and you received a long-term asset—land. So, there were low barriers to entry, and these absentee farmers didn't live with the consequences of their farming methods; they simply came and collected their profits.

The recent technological advances in our field have drastically reduced the cost of outreach to our clients. While most areas would use that moment to capture the cost efficiency and reduce headcount, we have increased the number of SDRs by 1,200 percent over the past five to seven years.[4] Instead of taking the efficiency gain and focusing on the effectiveness with reduced resources, we have exponentially increased our capacity to do outreach collectively, as an industry. Perhaps we can understand the decrease in per-salesperson productivity and quota attainment. This trend may have caused a corresponding 20 percent sales role decline over the past three years.[5] Forrester's report predicted this decline in 2015.[6] This decrease in effectiveness has led many organizations to double down on bad strategies.

But there is a trend that is even more worrisome. With the reduced cost of outreach, the barrier to entry for new companies to enter the business-to-business market segments has dropped. While a few companies have reduced their headcount and gained greater productivity, others have doubled down, and others have entered the market because of that low outreach cost. The SaaS explosion is an example—just take the marketing and sales tech explosions. Because of the reduced cost, companies can also cover more of their markets and develop higher cadence frequency. That means I can contact more people and do it more often with the same headcount. But I'm not the only one who does this; more players can enter the market now.

While some companies hold headcount steady, others increase their headcount. Over the past few years, this has led to a mania in sales hiring. At the same time, we have seen exponential advances in outreach capacity per salesperson. Meanwhile, the increased efficiency also expands the number of new players in the business-to-business market because of the reduced barrier to entry and perceived reduced cost of sales.

So, what could go wrong with this picture? Have the number of client companies in each market increased exponentially over the same period? What about the number of prospects we are targeting in those companies? Even with *The Challenger Sale*'s findings of 5.4–6.8 to 10–13 influencers in the buying process,[7] the growth in capacity for outreach is substantially more significant than the growth in prospects to contact. But we have increased the number of people doing this job exponentially, so the buyer is being overwhelmed with outreach. This sounds a little bit like the suitcase farmers, doesn't it?

I propose that we are in a modern Dust Bowl. Efficacy of effort continues to drop. Customers continue to report that they value sales contact less than in the past.[8] At the same time, because of low costs and mechanized outreach, almost anyone can become a suitcase go-to-market company, plow the customer base (land), then bring their suitcase and gather what profits they can and move on to the next opportunity. Meanwhile, the land (market segments), which is relied on by the people who have to sell into the market for their livelihoods, is becoming more and more fallow. What makes this a substantial constraint for legacy firms is that you have no control over your customer base or your white space. There is no way for you to protect your customers and prospects from modern-day suitcase farmers. Those who discover and deploy modern sales methods and motions will survive the Dust Bowl and will reduce the available profits for those suitcase farmers.

THE CUSTOMER PERSPECTIVE

Business and organizational buyers have already changed their expectations of the buying experience. As a buyer in their personal life, they have been FAANGMed. The vast majority of our buyers are now influenced by their social network—that's F, for Facebook. Apple—our A—has ensured that our mobile phones are an appendage, attached to each of us constantly. We check our phone for everything and expect it to answer just about any question we might have. The second A stands for Amazon, no longer just for books; it is for everything. We know we can find just about anything on the web, and most of us start with Amazon or other sites that have become the retail and wholesale mall in the cloud. We also expect it within 48 hours, and most likely, we want free shipping. Big-G Google is now in our homes, as voice search is making the sci-fi movies of the past century look like our present. We can search via our phone, the computer, or voice and have an endless library of information available at our command 24/7/365.

The consumer sector has been on top of these trends, if not making these markets. Meanwhile, these same consumers go to work and try to buy as business buyers, and they are sorely disappointed by the backward, low-tech version of sales they encounter. When they are shopping on Amazon, through an app on their Apple phone, for something they found on Google, they just click the button and expect it on their porch in 24–48 hours. Still, they have installed video surveillance on their front door. At work, they deal with internal procurement rules and vendor agreements, poorly designed websites, and the need to work through salespeople. They receive a barrage of messaging from the

1,200 percent increase of SDRs and the 10–50x amplification available to those SDRs. They are frustrated with business-to-business buying.

They don't get the same experience—*unless they do*. If they can find a similar experience at work as they do at home, guess where they choose to spend their money? You see, we really aren't that patient anymore; we have been FAANGMed, but most business-to-business buying processes are still pre-FAANGM. Those companies that develop and deploy frictionless experiences for their customers will reap a competitive advantage.[9]

As social creatures, buyers have lost their faith in expert information and recommendations; they prefer social data.[10] As consumers, we have had Yelp and Tripadvisor, and even Tinder. We know the customer ranking of our Uber driver. We expect that we can have accurate social ranking data in the business-to-business buying areas as well. Gartner has provided this service in the technology sector for many years on large purchases. In the technology sales stack arena, we have seen the emergence of G2 Crowd and Vendor Neutral to begin to provide neutral or social feedback on business-to-business technology purchases. LinkedIn and Twitter social posts also offer sources of feedback that the buyer demands. But most of these sources have yet to find a way to be unbiased and genuinely authentic. Who will meet the demand for trustworthy platforms of unbiased, authentic business-to-business information?

What Can We Learn?

- Organizations can experience 10–50 times the outcomes with proper deployment of technology. When combined with the buyer's or customer's preference for digital information and engagement, we should be able to increase the velocity of go-to-market strategies, with lower headcount.

- However, over 80 percent of the current market is following a classic sales machine model. When they deploy technology, they are mechanizing classic activities and tactics, which produce modern suitcase farmers, who are damaging white space for most companies.

- Buyers and customers are reducing their desire for and value of interaction with salespeople.

CHAPTER 3

THE MODERN EVOLUTION OF SALES

At the 2017 AA-ISP Leadership Summit in Chicago, a vice president of Microsoft gave the keynote presentation, showing what an organization can do when they build an inside sales organization from the ground up using modern methods, motions, and tools. The Dublin offices reported an eight- and tenfold performance increase year over year for average deal size and number of deals per quarter, respectively.[1] Later that year, I was allowed to tour the Dublin office to interview the sales leadership and team members at this site to confirm what I had heard at the presentation. To my surprise, their model was still being improved. This and other visits with the Microsoft Demand Generation team have shown that they continue to see significant improvements in critical key performance indicators (KPIs). In fact, in November 2019, at the UT Dallas Sales Leadership Summit, I interviewed another Microsoft leader from the same team, who shared that her organization had recently experienced a sixfold performance jump in the previous year with a single-digit global change in employees.[2] So clearly, multiplier effects are not only possible; they are happening right now.

When I teach my graduate class on digital sales strategy, identifying and evaluating the impact of innovations on the sales ecosystem helps us understand the past and the present and perhaps even the future of our field. So it may be helpful to review several significant innovations and evaluate how these innovations have changed buyers, sellers, and organizations. The early innovations may seem tedious but will help us develop a means to assess currently diffusing technologies and innovations in the early stage of adoption. This review of the past will allow us to set the stage and identify the key tools to resolve the sales innovation paradox and experience productivity similar to Microsoft's.

WEB 1.0

Believe it or not, businesses used the newspaper classifieds to advertise employment openings back in the day. While newspapers made substantial money from display advertising, the classified ads were a steady source of revenue. When you needed a job, you bought a newspaper and checked the classified ads. With the advent of the internet, Craigslist caused a significant change in the newspaper business model. Some research proposes that Craigslist caused over $5.4 billion in lost revenue for the industry, with between 40 percent and 70 percent of their revenues from classified ads lost.[3] The web changed the look of today's newspapers; we don't see many classified ads anymore. Craigslist is just one example of how the internet has changed one industry. The internet gave buyers and sellers new sources of information, new places to transact business, new places to advertise, and even new ways to communicate with electronic mail.

The opportunity for companies with the invention of the World Wide Web was to create a company website. Each business was able to create a digital storefront, brochure, billboards, and so on. The development of digital storefronts allowed local firms to become global and global firms to become local. Companies altered their behavior to take advantage of having their story and perhaps even their store open 24/7/365. These developments also changed the way consumers began to shop. As buyers started to learn more, they could browse company websites, research multiple vendors, become more informed, and perhaps bypass the need to call the company and ask for materials, thereby avoiding conversations with salespeople. With better-informed buyers, the salesperson's role was also different. With informed buyers, salespeople face more knowledgeable customers further down the buying journey, as is reported in *The Challenger Sale*.[4]

While individuals also developed personal landing pages, the business market now needed to create ways to get people to come to their websites. Many people in today's world would think of search as the best way, but at first, it was cumbersome. So lots of enterprising companies realized that they could develop content sites and sell advertising.

In 2005, Alex Tu came up with the million-dollar home page (www.milliondollarhomepage.com). He sold each pixel of his page for $1. Alex figured his site would gain enough attention that other companies would pay for a button on his webpage to help promote their websites. At first, people said he was crazy. However, you can see for yourself that he sold out all the pixels and made a million dollars. Although he was not the inventor of online ads, Alex proved that sites could generate ad revenue as their primary function. Naturally, this spawned thousands of content websites. Not only were websites created, but a new category of companies called *content aggregators* was born. These companies would pay writers to develop content. Then they would sell those stories to content publishers or use them on their own sites. The number of impressions (the number of times the ad was viewed) or the number of clicks generated the revenue. Some companies went so far as to develop commission structures for purchases from clicks, often referred to as *affiliate marketing agreements*.

Digital advertising and content outlets exploded during this time, so companies began to reallocate their ad spend. Some were able to better serve their customers via order-taking from their websites, which may have led to less reliance on salespeople for revenue. Consumers and corporate buyers now had even more sources of information. A new challenge arose: determining what was a good source of information versus a less reliable source, not to mention sifting through the digital noise and overwhelming amounts of data. The seller was facing a buyer with many sources of information that could lead to a more informed buyer or a more misinformed or confused buyer. At the same time, the idea of salespeople as thought leaders was emerging. Sales leaders and salespeople could also be writers and become experts in their field. This concept might blur the lines between sales and marketing.

Old and new media companies learned that websites could gain attention and sell display ads, links to other websites, and even classi-fied ads. With a low barrier to entry, anyone could create a website and try to gain attention like the content aggregators. This reality developed a natural challenge: how to get your website found.

Early search models categorized the internet; one early player was Yahoo! An alternative strategy emerged to allow users to search for what they wanted to find. Google became the winner of the search methods. Yahoo! had several opportunities to purchase Google. Of course, it is clear how that all worked out.

As Google matured, it provided analytics data to show the fre-quency of search terms and monetize its business by selling sponsored ads for search terms. Companies now could identify customers who were engaging in active search. Google's search results created search engine optimization, the concept of developing a website to become the top result on Google with targeted search terms. Likewise, compa-nies can now target advertising based on search terms and phrases. In theory, customers and buyers were able to find relevant content when they searched for information. They became more informed and more empowered to research competing market offerings, and they gained insights from third-party content sites. From a sales perspective, this further increased buyer knowledge. For those firms with sophisticated lead generation strategies, these web innovations led to more leads from their website. Naturally, more leads would create a greater need for more salespeople or better systems to process those leads. The sales and marketing departments had more opportunities to interact for better or for worse.

So let's go back for a moment to this concept of affiliate marketing and expand the idea a bit. If the affiliate marketer could become more efficient at display advertising, search marketing, or simply getting people to their site more efficiently, they could literally outbid the companies they represented. So marketplace websites came into being. Two distinct marketplaces are good examples—namely, eBay and Amazon. Anyone could list products for sale on eBay, which, at first, was primarily an auction website. At first, Amazon was a bookseller, which had more titles than most bookstores. However, Amazon soon realized that its strategy could go beyond just books. Move forward to the modern day, and we now have Amazon as one of the largest digital marketplaces. The concept of digital marketplaces like eBay and Amazon gave companies choices to open stores in these marketplaces and allow resellers to sell their products for them. Although this created new sources of channel conflict in the current moment, more sales were moving to digital with the online marketplaces. Customers could shop multiple vendors using one website (Amazon, eBay, and others). With more customers choosing online marketplaces, buyers' preferences were more likely to adapt from traditional salesperson interaction to digital engagement.

Although it is now hard to imagine a world without email, its adoption had a significant effect on the business-to-business marketplace. These days, most people have at least two email addresses—one personal and one for their work. With work emails, companies could now communicate with their employees and their customers 24/7/365 with essentially zero cost. We have seen both marketing and sales departments use email as a significant part of their outreach strategy to potential clients, prospects, and customers. On the customer side, your inbox is full of valuable and desired communication, as well as a lot of noise from people and companies you don't know or value. From a seller's perspective, email is a low-cost, high-volume method to reach out to prospects and communicate with existing customers.

The internet changed the world of business as we know it. Customers could search for and find essential information. Additionally, online marketplaces allowed buyers and sellers to transact digitally on their own time. And the ability to digitally communicate both asynchronously (email) and synchronously (chat) was now available. This accessibility changed the information asymmetry.

WEB 2.0

While Amazon and Alibaba became the winners in the online marketplace space, Facebook and LinkedIn won that battle in the social space. Although many used the internet to promote products, services, and causes, some people also developed personal websites. However, doing so was not overly intuitive at first; it required sufficient patience, time, and resources to build, host, and maintain your website. It seems natural that innovative minds would see this as an opportunity to simplify this process and add some functionality. MySpace and Facebook allowed people to create a personal website with limited time and resources. Although their sites were a bit crude in functionality at first, it was more cost efficient than creating your own site from scratch. The desire for privacy led to groups and pages being limited to "friends." From these humble beginnings, social networks were born. You could digitally interact with close friends or strangers from around the world. You could now post, comment, poke, wink, tag, and like on social platforms.

What started in the consumer space expanded. Business platforms arrived, including LinkedIn, Yelp, and Tripadvisor, to name a few. Other social platforms came, including Instagram, Snapchat, and Twitter, each with their unique take on social engagement. The advent of social provided new opportunities for buyers, sellers, and companies.

More specifically, social created a new environment for individuals and firms to traverse. A new channel opened to develop and deliver content, manage brands, allocate ad spend, and communicate. Organizations needed to move beyond a simple website; they needed to determine whether they should develop pages and storefronts on social platforms. Given that there were various social platforms, this question was not just whether to have a social presence but which social sites their customers used. The role of marketing expanded to developing social pages and social ad campaigns and determining how to influence the social discussion about your brand.

Not only did customers have one more channel to seek out information from companies, but they could also request information from other buyers and customers. Websites like Yelp and Tripadvisor encouraged ranking a business after a customer's purchase. Amazon and eBay allowed customers to rate their experience with each seller. Buyers could now gain additional information instead of relying on the company website or the salesperson.

Social marketing was an early business strategy in the new environment. Advertising on social platforms allows for a high degree of precision and effectiveness. But the concept of social selling has substantially changed sales. Social platforms provided intelligence to the seller about a buyer's company, profile, and network, as well as several ways to connect with their customers and potential customers. Since most employees have LinkedIn profiles, these profiles provide a valuable data source for the seller to gain context on both the buyer and the firm. Most profiles show the title of the person, how long they have been in their job, their job history (both in and outside the firm), as well as where they went to college and so much more.

Salespeople can have more context about a person they are meeting for the very first time. Likewise, they can look up a customer profile when they get inbound leads. This type of information is not just useful before a meeting; it can also provide valuable context before cold outreach. Better yet, since LinkedIn is a network, salespeople can discover whether their existing network is connected to their prospects. If such a connection exists, an introduction request is possible instead of cold outreach. Merrill Lynch recently made the news by suggesting that they would no longer have their trainees cold call and would have them seek introductions moving forward.[5]

Not only is this information available on individual buyers, but it is also available for all the people who work at a given firm. LinkedIn's premium products allow for modern motions as we can determine the company's size, headcount growth, headcount distribution, and many other searchable firmographics with tools made possible by aggregating data from individual profiles. Such data provide valuable intelligence and context to the seller before meetings and allow sellers and marketers to develop ideal customer profiles to allow for more precise outreach efforts.

Having so much context should enhance and personalize communication using the platform's messaging feature, so we have one more way to communicate with our potential client. But LinkedIn is unique here. While emails and phone lines may have a gatekeeper or admin, because a LinkedIn profile is personal and moves with a professional from job to job, most executive buyers tend to manage their own LinkedIn accounts and email. Not only could a seller reach out directly or through an introduction, but they may also be able to engage with the prospect or client by engaging with their articles and posts. Therefore, LinkedIn and other social networks have opened many different and effective means of meaningful connection with both existing and future clients.

THE SAAS EVOLUTION

Another major disruptor to the sales field has been cloud computing. Eventually, technology companies realized that they could deploy applications on the internet and social media platforms. This realization has been a significant disruption to the software industry, not to mention the hardware sector. Deploying software on the cloud has many advantages, including reducing the cost of installing and maintaining software on servers and individual computers. By hosting the software in the cloud, software updates can be made at any time. They are eliminating the expense of reinstalling software on every computer.

But this opened up even more from a competition and sales perspective. With a cloud delivery model, the concept of software as a service (SaaS) was born. This innovation involved how software was hosted, delivered, paid for, and sold. Before cloud-based software, most businesses would purchase a license for their software and maintenance and service agreements and would install the software on their machines, then upgrade when a new version of the software was released. But under the new model, updates could be made more frequently since there was no installation process on servers and desktops; it could just be updated in the cloud. So companies developed a service-based revenue model where customers paid for software monthly, by the number of users. This change substantially reduced the upfront cost of purchasing software.

The SaaS model provided new producer economics, including the reduced cost to enter the software market. You did not need to deploy software specialists to every server and every computer. The cost to your customer to try a new piece of software was drastically reduced, creating very different buying journeys and selling processes. Similarly, the cost to provide access to one additional company or individual user of this product became marginal. So a new tech company could allow trial usage of a product to both individuals and organizations, promoting digital acquisition versus costly salespeople. These changes led to a lower barrier to entry for new players in the software space. Just about anyone could start a new software business with websites and social media. With modern tools, they could inform their market much more efficiently than in the past.

From the buyer's perspective, with a free trial and lower initial financial commitment, technology purchases are less risky. Additionally, they could choose to try or purchase a SaaS product individually, even if the company decides not to adopt the technology on the corporate side. So, clearly, a product could achieve penetration from the ground up via organic growth or down from the top by the organization. Such decisions were not possible before SaaS because purchasing, installing, and maintaining software required significant on-premise hardware and IT support. The modern model allows buyers to do trials with several vendors and evaluate the functionality of each competitor, increasing the buyer's knowledge before a company's adoption.

The impact on sales is multidimensional. First, sales in the SaaS space would be different from sales in the traditional software sales space. SaaS vendors would need to consider their objectives, whether they were to obtain trials, individual purchases, or entire company purchases. Customers would now have more information than before when they evaluated SaaS companies in the same competitive space. A clear challenge here would be the cost of acquisition versus the revenue from the acquisition. If the objective was trial or beta testing, paying a salesperson commission would create losses, because the costs per trial or sale would be much greater than the revenue generated. Even with a company-wide purchase, the initial revenue would be much smaller than the legacy software install model that preceded it. The birth of a less costly, higher velocity role would be necessary. Cue the birth of the SDR and books like *Predictable Revenue*[6] and *The Sales Development Playbook.*[7]

These changes led to an explosion of software applications in the marketing and sales space. Several people have been documenting this explosion fueled by venture capital investment. The marketing tech landscape, with over 5,000 applications for marketing professionals, is documented by Scott Brinker.[8] Nancy Nardin (SBI) and Nicolas De Kouchkovsky keep a chronicle of the sales tech landscapes.[9] These innovations have changed how we reach our potential clients and how we sell these types of products to clients.

MOBILE

I know it's hard to believe that there was a time when all phones had a wire coming from a wall in your home. When first available, mobile phones were big and clunky and used only by important people or people who wanted to spend a lot of money. You had to pay for each minute you used.

In the early stages of mobile adoption, most people maintained their landlines. From a sales perspective, we added one more communication channel to contact both clients and prospects. On the organizational side, the ability to reach key team members or executives was highly desirable. Most businesspeople gave out their number sparingly and used their phones primarily for emergencies, especially during the era of extremely high per-minute charges. From a sales perspective, the ability to move from a pager to a phone was a big moment. Paging someone was tedious. At first, pagers only provided the phone number of the person who contacted you; then you had to hunt down a phone to call them. If you were on the road, it was a payphone. When prices became reasonable for mobile phones, salespeople saw the value in answering their phones no matter where they were. In the early stages of adoption, it would be rare to contact a prospect on their cell phone, because such a call would cost the customer, and those phone numbers were not widely circulated. This is something to think about when you consider how different customer segments (e.g., age) may feel about people calling them on their mobile phones.

The smartphone was a significant shift in the relationships people had with their phones. The invention of the iPhone was substantial. Adding music, email, and cell service onto one device changed usage. As of 2019, over 80 percent of the US market had a smartphone.[10] Not all regions of the world are at the same adoption rate, but most developed countries now use smartphones. The phone became a computer and a music delivery system and, now, a video delivery device, moving from a means of communication to a means of productivity and entertainment. We now see more and more people cutting off their landlines and cable.[11]

The first thing to consider about the modern mobile world is that the phone is no longer seen as a phone. It is a supercomputer in your pocket. You can see your personal email, your work email, and your favorite websites, videos, and social websites all on your phone with the swipe of a finger. Now, everyone knows and expects that everyone is accessible all the time. We moved from being able to use internet sites only at home or at work, where we could access our computers, to accessing websites all the time and on the go.

Each company now faces mobile customers with expectations. Companies made infrastructure investments to allow their customers to have a seamless experience, from computer to mobile. Substantial investments were made to update websites and enhance the mobile experience as more and more engagement from customers and stakeholders came from mobile devices. While video was always available from computers, mobile also increased the engagement value of video to communicate information to existing customers and potential clients.

Sales professionals now had a mixed bag. Not only were business-to-business customers available on their work computer and their office phone, but they were also technically more approachable via their smartphones. An email could be seen just about anytime, just about anywhere, not just when your client or prospect was sitting at their desk. Although calling a mobile before smartphones was a risky strategy, you now have competition from all the other functions on that smartphone. Someone could be listening to their favorite music while running or cycling, then—boom—in comes your call. When we consider that social sites are also consistently available, sales professionals have multiple channels to approach their clients—office phone, mobile phone, email, and social.

THE APP REVOLUTION

With smartphones diffused throughout the market, a new platform was available to expand the SaaS model, which created an explosion of applications. Although applications were developed before smart-phones (think of the Salesforce.com AppExchange and the social media application Farmville on Facebook), the diffusion of smartphones added another delivery mechanism. As we consider how the smart-phone launched an app revolution, we see converging forces creating multifaceted innovation.

All companies with websites now had to decide what investment to make. Do you invest in a mobile site, an application, or both? Naturally, as more and more companies developed easier to use websites to service their customers, creating an application became necessary to meet their customers' expectations.

A second company dimension was the concept that new SaaS com-panies could enter the market with multiple delivery channels to choose from, like social media sites, websites, app exchanges of other SaaS com-panies (e.g., the Salesforce.com AppExchange), or smartphones using the app stores hosted by Apple and Android. People could write code or pay coders to develop applications with minimal cost. Forming such SaaS offerings quickly and at a low cost and investing in these applica-tions and related companies created a whole new world of start-ups in both the consumer and business markets.

Not only has this changed the way we sell to customers, but it has also developed a whole market of technology companies that are selling applications to businesses. Before these trends, only the large software companies with substantial funding could enter the business-to-business market. Now, large software companies are the ultimate customer. Small technology firms work to develop recurring revenue and attract the interest of one of the larger technology firms like Salesforce, Adobe, or Google to purchase their application-based company. A whole industry has emerged to fund, build, and sell these technology companies.

This funding source has led to an app explosion in the marketing and sales tech landscapes. From a business standpoint, this has allowed different companies to invent point solutions, which augment or automate a specific task or customer interaction rather than developing a complete software solution. In the sales world, this has created what we call the *sales stack*: all the different point solutions that a salesperson or organization might stack on top of their CRM system or adjacent to their existing systems.

Most CRM companies developed the capacity to access your customer data on the go via mobile applications. Given Salesforce.com's application development ecosystem, many companies could provide applications that could also function on all devices supported by the hosting application. Depending on the cost of the application and corporate use policies, individual sales professionals could choose to use the corporation-provided sales stack or potentially augment the company sales stack with additional applications independent of the company. To take the time to discuss the impact of each sales application in Nancy Nardin's SalesTech Landscape[12] would be a book in itself. The deployment of mobile device applications continues to affect organizational and individual sales motions and go-to-market strategy implementations.

The sales and marketing technology application explosion also affected customers and buyers. Customers were able to transact with firms by using technology (applications) rather than interacting with humans. Today, we consume our media via applications, make transactions via applications, and can do just about everything else via applications. On the buyer's side, the sellers are now using more and more technology as they manage our buying process and reach out. We can begin to imagine how this might cause a sales innovation paradox or might have multiplying effects.

MOBILE REPRISE

As mobile technology has moved to 4G and 5G standards, our devices are better capable of delivering video. With each generation of mobile technology infrastructure, video delivery is becoming more affordable, and the quality and fidelity keep increasing. While our smartphones give us 24/7/365 access to entertainment, those devices also give us new methods for reaching out to our customers and delivering content. Companies like Zoom, Webex, MS Teams, and others are providing us with high-fidelity video calls on most devices, including mobile phones. The recent pandemic moved this to the mainstream.

Companies have used video to promote their brands since the advent of motion pictures, through television, and on to YouTube. As phone and laptop cameras have increased in quality, more and more applications have either incorporated video or become stand-alone video applications that allow more video delivery of sales messaging, not just marketing. This increase in mobile capability has led more and more companies to invest in video call technology. Social media platforms have moved to provide live streaming services, including Facebook Live and LinkedIn Live. We can also record video and send it to friends and clients. Early indicators are that these videos are more effective than other forms of sales communications like voicemail and emails. The impact of video on the buyer-seller relationship in the business-to-business sector is currently diffusing, and its effect has yet to be rigorously measured.

ARTIFICIAL INTELLIGENCE

For quite some time, we have been able to program computers to automate sales motions and thereby increase the efficiency of the sales force. Today's environment is full of companies claiming to use AI, but they simply use programmed algorithms. However, there are some very useful deployments of machine learning in the sales space that will likely have a lasting impact on the field. Many homes use voice technology like Siri on Apple phones, Alexa, and Google Home. This innovation shows us that voice recognition is sufficiently advanced to allow a computer to interpret a human voice. In the sales world, IBM Watson has several sales-related tools that can translate voice to text, analyze tone, and even predict your personality profile.[13]

Gong and Chorus.ai (acquired by ZoomInfo.com in 2021) are positioning to create a new category called *conversation intelligence*, using voice to text and related AI. xiQ has developed the ability to determine personality profiles based on a Google search of a person's name and build a company dossier using AI search technology. Microsoft and Salesforce have developed predictive algorithms based on programming and machine learning to develop predictive lead scoring and predictive pipeline analysis. Companies are automating campaigns for prospects to build a sales version of marketing automation called *sales engagement*, a new sales technology category.

We are close to having machine learning and automated algorithms that could find our target market, nurture that market with campaigns, and score the lead to the point of booking revenue or making a phone call for the salesperson, who is then prompted with the customer history of the client and a list of their needs. After the meeting, it could provide the notes of the meeting, develop the follow-up email, send the calendar invite for the next meeting, provide the necessary collateral, and watch the customer's engagement with both your collateral and content, as well as show any engagement with competitors' assets. Additionally, it could alert us when people in the buying committee have been promoted or left their company or when new members join the team. We are truly close to a point where our ability to witness the buyer's touchpoints with our company and our competitors can amplify what can be done by a salesperson.

A NEW WORLD

We are in a new world of sales and customer interaction. As buyers, we expect more from companies and salespeople. We have more information. Our access to and engagement with the technology change our access to information and how we communicate with others, including our customers. Sales organizations have more tools and information at their disposal. They have multiple ways to deliver messages to customers and determine the status of their customers' buying process. Technology has truly changed the landscape of how we engage and transact business. It has changed how we do sales and what our customers expect from us.

But a few key questions remain: Have sales processes changed? Furthermore, have sales organizations changed? More challenging: How can we develop an executable strategy when technology is still causing our organizations, our salespeople, and our buyers to change as we are trying to adapt? This rapid change is behind the sales innovation paradox. It is important to understand the changes and adapt as the market is adapting. Many companies are doing this well, and seeing how their strategies succeed can help your own sales expand. The current giants of the field are adapting and harnessing these innovations to experience exponential revenue gains, a multiplier effect!

What Can We Learn?

- With the advent of mobile, social, and apps, the available mediums of communication have been expanded for marketing and sales messaging.

- With the apps on social, mobile, and cloud-based platforms, barriers to entry have been reduced.

- Artificial intelligence and other technology give us more visibility on both the buying and the selling side of transaction in business-to-business.

CHAPTER 4

THE BUYER AND TECHNOLOGY

The Amazon team deployed a *long-tail strategy*. Amazon.com started as a bookstore when most bookstores would only carry top-selling books. In the brick-and-mortar days of retail, other specialty bookstores might have top-selling books and specialize in hard-to-find books or specific topics, such as children's or technical books. The internet gave specialty bookstores a broader audience and gave their market segments more places to find their product. This is where Amazon's strategy came into play: What if they became the online bookstore with the most titles? Why not all of them? They would sell the rare books and the bestsellers (and then they would decide which were the bestsellers). They would be able to reduce customer acquisition costs by gaining brand awareness and advertising efficiency. Furthermore, customers would reduce their search costs with Amazon's one-stop shopping.

As Amazon carried more and more books and hosted more and more booksellers' marketplace offerings, they could better satisfy customers' demand. The formation of an online website with a long tail of inventory was the innovation. However, the innovation makes no impact on the market until customers learn about it and choose to try it. If all a customer does is buy one book at Amazon and never come back, nothing interesting has happened. Amazon is just one more store in the market. As customers found value in the long-tail strategy, they began to alter their book-searching strategy. At first, this meant that they might choose to look at Amazon early in their search process. Eventually, some customers and some market segments started their search on Amazon, whereas other market segments searched only on Amazon. They have not only tried out the innovation but also adopted the new method of searching for and buying books. When customers adopt this search pattern, they do so for most or all their book purchases, not just the hard-to-find books.

Technology adoption leads to buyer behavioral changes, including actions, expectations, and demands. The pattern can then repeat itself and become a cycle. Identifying this pattern and tracking the cycles will help us better dissect the sales innovation paradox.

PHASE 1: ADOPTION AND DIFFUSION

With each new innovation, the critical first step is whether it will be adopted or whether it will be just a fad. The innovation itself doesn't start a pattern; the adoption does. Going to Amazon the first time does not mean that the customer has adopted a new way of shopping. Adoption of the Amazon model means that the customer often searches Amazon for their buying needs. On the other extreme is the concept of buying an essential product, like a smartphone, for the first time. Although it is possible that the smartphone user would tap out a text once and never use it again, consistent use is more likely. If you are starting to think, *But did they ditch the pager; set up the email feature, the music library, and their social media; and use the camera?* then you are starting to see the pattern. It is not sufficient for the smartphone to have the features (phone, text, music, email, etc.); individual users must try and then adopt those features. Technological innovation is important, but adoption of the innovation is what alters a market and its actors.

Most experts indicate that technology diffuses in an S shape. At first, very few people adopt the technology; this is the group of people who like to try new things, the early adopters. After that, we enter the exponential portion of the diffusion: The early and late majorities are the following two segments. Naturally, the last group is called the *laggards*.

Clearly, not all innovations diffuse to the whole marketplace. Likewise, some concepts, products, or services diffuse at different velocities. You could also imagine that some innovations might diffuse differently depending on various demographic variables (e.g., age, geography). Although whole books have been written about product diffusion and adoption,[1] we are more interested in seeing how the adoption of innovations might change an organizational buyer's behavior, including their actions, expectations, and the related demands of companies that sell to them.

PHASE 2: ADAPTATION

Adoption means that the customer has actually changed their behavior. A trial is one thing, but the behavior change is the signal that adoption has occurred. As someone goes to Amazon for books, they have changed their shopping motions and patterns. They no longer need to jump in the car to search the various bookstores for hard-to-find books or search different websites. Although some buyers may search Google at first, some will just skip that step and go right to Amazon. As more bookstores put their inventory online and others post their merchandise on Amazon storefronts, the depth of adoption for the consumer goes deeper as Amazon develops a broader inventory with price competition that didn't exist before.

For an early adopter of Amazon book purchases, the adoption was quite simple. You went to Amazon to buy books. But if you move forward to today's Amazon, we start to see that adoption can also be quite complex. Amazon didn't just stop at books; they realized that their model would work with other products as well. So in the modern day, when a new shopper discovers the Amazon marketplace, there is a lot to process. Today's Amazon has books, electronic books, entertainment, web services, home products, and just about everything else.

When multiple products, services, or product features are available, we need to look at adoption in terms of depth and breadth: the number of products, services, or attributes that a customer adopts from the company and how deep in the singular product, service, or feature they adopt. Although this might get confusing and might feel irrelevant, we need to remember that we are interested in the behavioral shift caused by the individual buyer's adaptation, caused by their adoption. The degree of adaptation is directly related to the depth and breadth of adoption. Furthermore, adaptation is not constant. As customers develop deeper and broader adoption, they will adapt their behavior.

At the individual buyer level, we are talking about a dynamic process rather than a static one. As we aggregate at the market level, the underlying market of buyers and consumers is in a continual process of adoption and related adaptation, which creates a market that is constantly shifting. This point is critical in cracking the sales innovation paradox: Your addressable market is continuously adapting to all the various technological innovations that they adopt.

PHASE 3: EXPECTATION

As we adopt technological innovation and adapt our behavior, we also may change our expectations, and in some instances, we demand the next iteration of innovation. As a buyer starts achieving success at Amazon for various books and other products, the customer may begin to expect to find all the books and products they need at Amazon. These buyer expectations can transfer to Amazon's competitors. Amazon provides two-day delivery for Prime members and is now working on getting to 24-hour delivery. Does the buyer now expect that same delivery service from all shopping online? When an Amazon customer doesn't pay for shipping with Prime, they also transfer this expectation to other online marketplaces and expect all companies to provide free shipping and other services.[2]

The invention of Wi-Fi allows us to have internet access without wiring. As this innovation entered our homes, offices, and businesses, we began to expect it to be available everywhere. And, suddenly, it is. More and more public places and businesses have Wi-Fi, not to attract customers but because customers expect it. Airlines provide Wi-Fi on more and more flights (now if we can just get the cruise ships to see the light). When this happens, we can see that the demand cycle leads to new product innovation or product extensions to allow for further adoption, adaptation, expectation, and demand cycles.

We see this pattern over and over again. For example, the release of the iPhone was quite a moment of technological innovation. In many ways, companies like Apple have created the expectation that products will get better with each new version, so naturally, with each new version of smartphones, we expect more features and more innovation. As we get more and more devices, we expect those devices will communicate seamlessly. People naturally see an innovation and then begin to ponder the next step in the innovation cycle. After we conceive it, we demand the next innovation to come soon.

Those technology firms who develop innovation for consumers create demand and markets for their products and services. They tend to be the trendsetters and market makers. This speed of innovation and creativity rarely transfers over to our work environments at the same rate. While innovation and progress wow consumers, they go to work and see organizational reality on full display. Disappointment can set in as those buyers expect innovation but do not see it in the business-to-business market as much as they see it in their homes. It often takes years to see the same level of innovation at the organizational level. I hope you start to see that this cycle might contribute to the sales innovation paradox. Business-to-business buyers develop expectations from their consumer purchases and interactions. When these expectations are not met, the industrial buyer may disengage or develop disappointment.

A clear example is the customer experience. Technology enables frictionless and seamless customer experiences. It can enhance most of our commercial interactions. Connecting all the technology to make such an experience possible is more challenging in a business than in a home. But it doesn't change our expectation that such an experience is possible. Those who achieve these experiences before their competitors will obtain an advantage, assuming they can make these changes profitably.[3]

THE TABS CYCLE

While innovation creates an expectation for more and more innovation, actual innovation often changes us as we engage with it. This is called the *technology adoption and behavioral shift* (TABS) cycle (see figure 4.1).

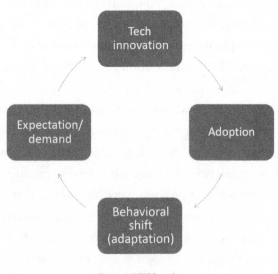

Figure 4.1 TABS cycle.

Apple

I know it is hard to believe, but computers didn't always operate with touchscreens, trackpads, or even a mouse. Back in the day, they didn't even have easy-to-use menus. Nope, computers were DOS-based. For those of you who weren't alive at the time, DOS was all text, usually green on a black background. You had to type in commands. It was brutal. Computers were not overly accessible. They were expensive and required quite a bit of technical knowledge to use. In 1984, Apple, then a small company, launched a brand-new product called the Macintosh. It had a graphical user interface (the menus and icons you use now) and a mouse to navigate that interface.

The Macintosh was a game changer. Its ease of use allowed for mass distribution of computing power. Anyone could now own a computer, and it was much simpler to use than its competitors. Not only did this change the consumer market for computers, but it also changed the productivity of businesses as more and more people were able to learn to use computers. It expanded the market for computers into many more segments beyond big business. Even small businesses could own a computer and obtain the associated productivity gains. We moved from typewriters—which were cumbersome and hard to correct—to personal computers, which changed workers' lives and even saved time for college students writing essays and papers.

Apple developed the iPod in 2001. Sony had developed the Walkman, which allowed music on the go, but the iPod leaped into making music digital and portable for the masses. When Apple introduced the iPod, it also introduced the Apple Music Store, so music could be purchased online and played on the device. Overnight, people began paying for the music that they were previously (illegally) downloading for free. The uniqueness, cool factor, and quality of sound were sufficient to change the behavior of many consumers and changed the way music was monetized.

However, it wasn't just the consumers who changed via this innovation. The Apple Music Store also removed a barrier to entry for musicians. A band or singer no longer needed to get a record label to distribute their music to stores. They could record the music themselves and send it to Apple. This disruption substantially changed the music industry and how new music artists became famous.

In 2007, Apple invented the iPhone. This device combined phone, email, and music in one device, and it changed everything. From the Macintosh came the iPod and then the iPhone; each Apple innovation set the stage for the next. As behaviors changed, the demand for innovation was ready for the next new product.

After the successful launch of the iPhone, Apple innovated again by launching the App Store. Using an app rather than a website allowed companies to create a more consistent user experience on Apple devices. With this new store, another barrier to entry dropped: Anyone who learned Apple's mobile development language could develop an application and sell that application in the App Store. A whole new marketplace formed, which created more consumer demand for more apps—and the TABS cycle continues.

In 2010, Apple introduced the iPad. This product was positioned between an iPhone and the relatively large and cumbersome laptop computer. The smartphone had changed the way people used their phones to the point that they were using them as portable computers. There was a demand for an iPhone that was like a computer, hence the iPad. For laptop computer manufacturers, this created new demand for devices that were smaller and sleeker. And the iPad screen, larger than a smartphone's but nearly as portable, provided all new opportunities to develop applications. The TABS cycle began anew in this market: More and more use cases arrived for iPads, an innovative cycle that we still witness today.

Siri uses AI to listen to voice commands and has become a major point of search. Apple also invented the Apple Watch in 2015, which combined the previous innovations of the iPhone but moved to a wearable device with a much smaller screen. Although wireless earphones have existed for a long time, Apple made them crucial by removing the previously ubiquitous headphone jack from most of their mobile devices. And they released AirPods to fill the market gap they had created. In today's world, someone can be running or cycling, having their heart monitored by their watch, and can ask Siri to play motivational workout music through their AirPods. We can see from all these innovations the depth and breadth of Apple's products and how adoption will lead to new behavioral patterns and desires for the next level of innovation.

Google

Google has changed consumer behavior with its innovations in search, video, mobile, and voice. The company's early innovation was making it easier to discover information on the internet. Before Google, navigating was less easy, and there were many less effective search engines. Before that, we had to go to the library or look in a book called an *encyclopedia*. Salespeople used to go door to door and sell encyclopedias, as that was how a home would have access to basic information. We quit buying encyclopedias, and now those sales jobs are gone. We just Google it. When we are in a conversation and wonder about a fact, it is not uncommon for someone to pause and look at their phone to find a point related to the discussion. In sales today, a potential client can find information about your company, your competitors, and your existing customers' reviews of your product, all via search.

While Google didn't create the video as a platform, they purchased YouTube[4] and have continued to own both of the largest areas of the search market, text and video. Video is the second-largest search engine in the world.[5] With video available on demand anytime, anyplace with mobile, we consume it at a higher and higher rate. YouTube changed where we got our entertainment. At first, it was more commercial content, but now we have YouTube stars, including a boy who is worth tens of millions for his videos of opening toys.[6] People spend more time watching videos on their devices than watching TV, and there is more content to choose from.[7]

We have discussed the impact of applications for business, but applications have also changed consumers' behavior. The Android operating system was created in 2008 by Google for use on various devices, including mobile phones. Google counterpunched to compete with Apple and developed its own app store, Google Play. Google Maps has changed the way we navigate and destroyed the market for stand-alone GPS navigation systems. Google Home uses Google Assistant to answer questions spoken aloud and to interact with other smart devices in your house. You can turn on your lights, start your coffee maker, or even light up your grill with voice commands. We are in the early stages of this technology and its commercial use. As these devices become more commonplace, we will see more demand in the mobile space, in our vehicles, and at work.

Microsoft

Microsoft has been a significant technology player since its inception. Their operating systems have consistently led them to market domination. When Apple developed their user interface, they only allowed their operating system to be used on Apple computers. However, Microsoft used a different strategy. They allowed any computer to use their operating system. They also tailed the Macintosh with Windows, which made them more accessible and user-friendly without the need for training on DOS commands. The ability to connect computers to networks began to change the workforce's productivity, especially as Windows-based computers became more widely available, affordable, and accessible.

With Windows, people wanted more productive and efficient ways to perform tasks like developing documents, storing data, doing computations, and creating presentations. Naturally, companies developed word processors, databases, spreadsheets, and presentation software.

Eventually, Windows gave Microsoft the edge to launch their own products to perform these functions, and they gave us the Office suite of products, including Word (for word processing), Access (databases), Excel (spreadsheets), and PowerPoint (presentations). By bundling these products into a single suite and, in some cases, adding a sample license with new computers, they could solidify their position as a market leader. The TABS cycle led from hardware to operating system to software, and Microsoft continues to reap the benefits.

Innovations from Microsoft opened up computing to the masses. The early battle between Apple and Microsoft for the personal computer market was instrumental in bringing us to the moment we are now in. With some historical context, the cycle of innovation, adoption, adaptation, expectation, and demand for more innovation becomes clear.

What Can We Learn?

- As consumers and corporate buyers, we expect to find what we need on the internet anytime, anywhere.

- We desire and expect a frictionless, digitally enhanced experience because we know it is technologically feasible.

- I don't want to talk to you until I do; then I want you to respond immediately and be available 24/7/365.

- I can buy and learn about your products just fine from your website, so show me how interaction with your team will add value to my purchase decision.

- New buyer segments are forming with each innovation. These segments are based not only on adoption but also on the buyer's corresponding behavioral shift, which is directly related to both the depth and the breadth of adoption.

CHAPTER 5

THE SELLER AND TECHNOLOGY

A n innovation can be adopted at the consumer level, the worker level, or the organizational level. The same consumers who inadvertently contribute to the TABS cycle go to work and find value in innovation in their professional roles. Specifically, TABS affects sales professionals in the business-to-business market just like it does general consumers.

Although sellers are consumers at home, their actions at work represent a team, a company, and a brand. As consumers, they can use Alexa, Google Home, or Siri to ask which stores and restaurants are open, or they can start their grill or smoker, lock the front door, turn off the lights, vacuum the living room, or even mow the lawn with a voice command. Indeed, the technology exists that would allow a salesperson to ask the same voice-enabled AI to find an addressable market for your product, determine the appropriate ideal customer profile, and start a proper sequence. And why not just see who is available to take your call right now so that you can be a highly efficient salesperson? But although the tech is there, this service is not widely available.

Adopting a technology at home is a pretty straightforward decision.

You learn about the technology, you assess its value to you, and you determine whether you have sufficient resources (money to purchase and time to learn how to get value out of the purchase). Then you make a purchase and begin your adoption journey.

As a salesperson, you learn about an innovation that might make you more efficient. You assess its value and determine how your adoption of this technology would enhance or detract from your organization's current strategies and policies. In addition, you determine how adopting this technology might affect your standing within the organization. Purchasing and adopting a piece of technology might also require that you run this idea by your sales manager, sales enablement team, sales operations team, sales technology team, and any number of other stakeholders.

So let's say that you clear the sales team hurdle and you are clear to proceed. Now we are on to the resource considerations. Do you have budget authority, or can you get reimbursed for the purchase? Does the technology require integration with the company's CRM, sales force automation (SFA), and other sales stack components to make the investment worth your consideration? What is the learning curve, and do you have the time to get up to speed on the new technology? Are you feeling a bit overwhelmed yet? Let's just add, if things go wrong, that you don't just lose the money you spent and the time invested; your poor use of the technology may affect your team, your boss, and your company. So, at best, you are embarrassed if you make a mistake. At worst, you get fired because of the way the technology was used or deployed.

And we are only talking about adopting the technology for your own use. What if you were considering this technology for your team, your department, or the whole company? Well, it doesn't take long to see why organizational buying decisions are not the same as consumer buying decisions, as shown in figure 5.1. The purchase process is clearly different, not to mention the actual adoption. Corporate adoption of technology is hardly guaranteed. The more complex the technology, the

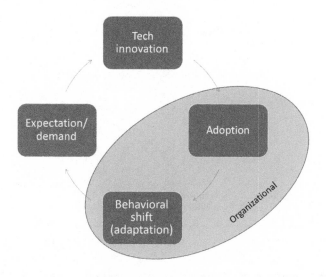

Figure 5.1. Organizational TABS cycle.

greater the depth and breadth of adoption issues that will determine the degree of adaptation. Now we are moving into the subject of organizational change.

The challenge and the opportunity here is that the technology exists to generate greater productivity in sales, but the sales community is not harnessing the same technology to automate and augment their tasks. The business-to-consumer sector has not only figured this out, but they also continue to be ahead of the business-to-business market. The relative lack of agility and increased risk to organizations compared to individual consumers lead to slower adoption.

Many organizations are aware of Gartner's famous hype cycle (see figure 5.2). It starts when the promise of adopting technology brings a hyped level of new benefits.[1] However, most tech companies cannot deliver on the hype, or they cannot adapt to the technology. At this early stage, both innovators and adopters discover the attributes of the innovation and their relative value. We then enter Gartner's trough of disillusionment—where the overall market realizes that the hype was overblown—then the slope of enlightenment, followed by the plateau of

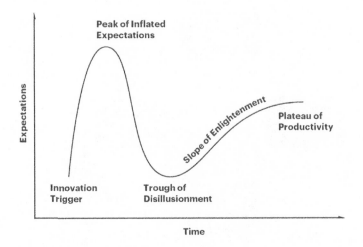

Figure 5.2. Gartner hype cycle. (Source: Gartner, "Gartner Hype Cycle," accessed June 14, 2022, https://www.gartner.com/en/research/methodologies/gartner-hype-cycle.)

productivity. With executive leadership knowing about the hype cycle, their organizations can develop a more cautious approach to technology innovation and its eventual adoption. Those organizations large enough to employ IT professionals to support their infrastructure will be more careful when adopting new technology if they have experienced the hype cycle with previous organization-level technology adoptions.

Sales organizations, however, are unique in their willingness to innovate to accomplish their objectives with greater efficiency and efficacy, because those incentives are most often directly aligned with revenue. Although the buyer uses technology to change the way they gain information and buy, the seller looks to increase the speed and effectiveness of their efforts to sell products and services. Therefore, we see salespeople adopting technology individually or in small groups, and the sales organization as a whole moves much slower. Only in rare instances would we see a sales organization agile enough to adopt technology at the same rate consumers do.

Although early technology innovations were focused on databases to manage customer relationships and govern resources (enterprise resource planning), modern sales technology looks at the overall sales funnel as the design point. Marketing's influence is apparent as many organizations use marketing's AIDA model: awareness, interest, desire, action.[2] The sales funnel moves from lead identification to a meeting, closing on the deal, and account management for ongoing relationships. It is not uncommon to have organizations operate with dual funnels, one to move a customer from prospect to a marketing qualified lead or sales accepted lead, and the other to move from qualified lead to purchase.

Given the system in place, the technology sector has developed innovative products and services to automate and augment both of these funnels. Chiefmartec.com maintains an infographic of these technologies with over 8,000 different applications as of 2021. Nancy Nardin and Nicolas De Kouchkovsky maintain documentation of the emerging sales tech landscape of over 1,100 technology applications for the sales field.[3] The marketing automation field focuses on the consumer market, whereas SFA focuses on organizational buying or the business-to-business market.

In the business-to-business market, marketing and sales need to collaborate. This collaboration is also essential for those who sell products to retail and other channels. In the consumer market, marketing tends to significantly influence the strategic direction, given that a market research team would own the data on consumer trends. However, in the business-to-business market, the sales force's daily interaction with the customer gives the sales organization direct access to the voice of the customer. This difference often leads us to discuss the strategy to align marketing and sales, and there is sufficient research that supports that value.[4]

PUTTING SALES TECHNOLOGY TO USE

The primary and necessary elements of a sales technology portfolio are the sales stack. Most organizations start with the foundation of the CRM platform. These products allow a company to manage the data related to the customer. Given that sales organizations work with both customers and potential customers, most sales organizations use CRM extensions or operate in concert with SFA systems, which organize all the sales interactions made with contacts in one accessible data source.

The next basic technology would be a source of leads. Although mailing lists and directories have been around for decades, data sources now need to include name, address, title, office phone, email, mobile phone, and even social media information. However, we can even get more precise lead intelligence in today's market because of the vast amounts of data available on individuals and organizations. Additionally, sales organizations need to be able to do sales forecasting. Most CRM and SFA tools have report functions that allow us to develop forward-looking and backward-looking reports. The need to create an accurate forecast for publicly traded firms can't be understated. We must either hire capable people to develop these forecasts or use tools that will make those forecasts from the available data.

Once they have the essential foundational technologies, organizations usually add to their sales stack. Nancy Nardin, from Smart Sales Tools, has organized 1,100 companies into 39 different types.[5] She chose the following major categories:

- Who to sell to and why

- How to engage and when

- Why they should buy, and from you

- What to do to close

- How to up- or cross-sell and renew

- How to manage, compensate, train, onboard, reinforce, and coach

Nicolas De Kouchkovsky bins over 950 companies into 41 different types.[6] He used the following major categories for his landscape:

- Engagement

- Productivity and enablement

- Sales intelligence

- Pipeline and analytics

- People management

The degree of innovation in our field has been rich and has grown exponentially over the past few years. There are now thousands of SaaS sales stack options to automate or augment the motions of individual salespeople or the organization as a whole. Companies and individuals have unlimited combinations of sales technology stack configurations from which to choose.

When you combine existing sales methods, strategies, and motions with modern sales tech, you get amplification.

PUTTING THIS ALL TOGETHER

What would happen if we combined all the various efficiency and automation technologies available to sales? The company database would be clean, accurate, and up to date. We could develop appropriate messaging and use AI to build personalized and situationally viable email messaging at scale. Dialers could ensure that we were talking to people when we use the phone, instead of wasting time dialing. Sales engagement tools and AI predictive analytics could identify where a salesperson should spend their time using the appropriate medium of communication, the correct messaging for the customer's situation, and the proper tone for their personality style. We could use AI to scan internal and external data points to determine who to nurture with our advertising—surrounding those customers with appropriate content relevant to their customer journey. Furthermore, these systems could determine who in our lead database needs or wants our product and services.

We live in a world where automation of redundant sales motions and functions is possible. We can augment sales professionals' required motions with data, context, and just-in-time messaging, coaching, and prioritization. If this could be put together and executed with proper targeting and messaging, we would see exponential performance from our sales organizations.

We would see a reduction in the need for salespeople and a different sales organizational structure. We would see more digital capture of revenue for the more simplistic purchases. We would see more ability to move down-market to previously unprofitable market segments. We would see new product life cycles accelerating. We would see product failures exposed much earlier and product success uncovered in shorter times. We would see faster innovation cycles because of the more efficient customer feedback loops. We would see more spending on technology, marketing, and sales support.

We would see higher overall compensation for the few salespeople we would still need. We would need to hire people who could engage with all these functions. Perhaps we would need to hire entirely different sales personalities. We would train and recruit differently. We would be in a different world. We would grow without headcount expansion. We would experience growth as a result of innovation in products and more effective messaging.

Can we perform with one or two SDRs, where we used to require 50–100? Microsoft answers this question with their demand response team's journey. Starting with the Dublin experience, they wanted to see what they could do if they unleashed all the modern technologies available and hired differently. From launch to 18 months, they experienced 800 percent funnel growth and 1,000 percent revenue growth in their first round.[7] But they didn't stop there. By focusing on what is possible, they increased performance by another 600 percent in 2019.[8] They continue to innovate.

Microsoft was able to harness technology innovation and adoption and adapt organizationally to improve its overall performance. So what is going on with the rest of the market? The breadth and depth of adoption comes to mind when we see different outcomes in the ecosystem. Not all adaptations lead to efficiency gains, especially when adoption is not universal and only some technologies' functionality is understood or adopted. For example, when deploying top-of-funnel strategies without much thought for down-funnel consequences, we might experience insufficient coverage to handle the increase in top-of-funnel success. These issues might explain why the majority of the market has decided to double down with a 1,200 percent increase in SDRs over the past few years.[9] The potential concern is that these SDRs have access to amplifying technology. Although they may not have all the technology we've imagined here, they are likely deploying parts of the technology stack that allow them to intensify their efforts at outreach. But the increased number of SDRs is evidence that we are not deploying the technology in a way that leads to greater productivity. Have we increased the number of SDRs because the amount of noise has reduced the efficacy of effort?

Sales and marketing technology innovation is behaviorally modifying organizations. While we should see more examples like Microsoft, we see more organizations increasing headcount and amplifying messaging. As stated by CSO Insights and other sources, the end effect is not an increase in productivity per sales headcount but a decrease in performance against quota.[10] So we see the sales innovation paradox is growing, not shrinking.

What Can We Learn?

- Adoption of technology is different at work than at home. Therefore, we see different diffusion patterns between the consumer and the organizational buying markets.

- With modern technologies and opportunities, we will need modern sales methods and motions. This will require new skills, new enablement, and perhaps different types of people to enter sales.

- The results of harnessing technology are exponential, if deployed properly. This will allow for lower headcount and greater go-to-market velocity.

- Having a sales organization that seizes the modern potential will allow for market dominance and greater market coverage (even into previously unprofitable segments).

CHAPTER 6

THE SELLER AND THE BUYER

Although buyers do contact sellers for inbound sales, this scenario is of less interest in explaining the sales innovation paradox. It is also not typical for the buyers to develop a strategic cadence plan, a strategic marketing plan, or sales funnels to make a purchase. But this is precisely what is happening when the seller considers their plan to prospect for potential clients and manage their buyer's journey through their marketing funnel, sales funnels, and internal sales pipeline.

THE BUYER'S JOURNEY

The buyer's journey often refers to the customer and their journey toward finding a solution, choosing to purchase a solution from a specific vendor to solve their particular problem. Of course, this very description is biased in its portrayal of a customer because it assumes the buyer is aware of their need and is acting on that awareness.

Let's start with that assumption for now. As you're very aware now, the buyer has developed expectations because of their own TABS cycle. They expect that sales firms will be efficient and will allow them to gather information efficiently and effectively and purchase effortlessly, just like they can do in their life as a consumer.

Meanwhile, the seller is sitting amid a technology-enhanced world with greater customer touchpoint transparency and the ability to amplify their efforts in a modern sales world. Technology exists to allow the seller to see all the customer's interactions in their buying journey both internally (for focal company's data) and externally (via cookies and AI tools). Successful journeys end at the same point: a purchase by the customer and a win by the team that secured the revenue.

The buyer's journey is the path a particular person or organization takes to the purchase. It is distinct for each customer. For example, it is different for a consumer purchase versus an organization purchase. When a consumer makes a purchase, they are focused on their needs and constrained by their resources, including the financial resources available for purchases. Organizational buyers, on the other hand, have other considerations. By definition, organizational buyers are purchasing on behalf of the needs and demands of the organization. Their part in this journey may be out of duty, or they may be directly vested in the value that the product or service may provide. Although consumer purchases may have more than one decision maker,[1] organizational procurement processes are often determined by numerous stakeholders.

Although the buyer's journey for a consumer and an organization may differ, organizational buyers are still TABS-modified consumers. Early technology innovations began in the corporate market and eventually filtered into the consumer market. But now that technology is more affordable and broadly diffused, we often see that innovations and behavioral shifts occur in the consumer sector first and then take some time to affect the organizational buyer-seller relationship. But since all organizational buyers are consumers, they may expect the same innovation they are experiencing in the consumer market, at work.

For example, when Amazon started moving beyond books, it started developing consumer storefronts. At one point, major retailers set up storefronts on Amazon, such as Target and Toys "R" Us, to reduce the expenditure of creating their sites and capture the growing popularity of Amazon.com. Move forward to the current moment, and you can purchase just about anything at online marketplaces, including airplane replacement parts on Alibaba. So we can see a clear example of organizational buying following the digital trend of online marketplaces established initially in the consumer market.

There are reasons for the delay in innovation and behavioral shift in business markets relative to the consumer market. Businesses have organizational objectives, whereas consumers have personal objectives. Those objectives may or may not match the individuals' goals, objectives, responsibilities, and career plans influencing an organizational buying decision and journey. The risks and rewards do not always align between the employee or influencer and the firm employing them. Selling into these environments requires an understanding and adjustment to these various complexities. The buying influencer models described in *New Strategic Selling*[2] and *The Challenger Customer*[3] are two great sources of complex decision-making to understand these points.

To summarize, a buyer's journey is as simple as becoming aware of a product, searching for it, developing a consideration set, determining the choice parameters, and then making a choice.[4] Using the jobs-to-be-done framework,[5] Gartner has done significant work on buyer enablement, showing that the organizational buying process has become complex for more significant deals. Many sources now indicate that the number of influencers has increased over the years. So, clearly, when an organization makes a decision, there are many people involved and many jobs to be done before the organization can commit to a purchase.

Although these models are helpful, do they help us understand the buyer's actual journey from a seller's perspective? Most often, they lead us to a touchpoint analysis of how our actions will guide our customers to the next stage in our sales process and therefore provide no mapping to an actual customer journey. Those who influence the buying decision do not get up each day and consider their next step in the framework. Similarly, buyers don't think about your sales process either. These influencers think about many things, like their projects, deliverables, and work to get done for their promotion, paycheck, and bonus. When you are fortunate enough that your product or service is relevant to their actual focus, you may be relevant to their buyer journey. Otherwise, you are a distraction. The organization's buyer's journey is quite complex.

ALIGNING THE BUYER'S AND SELLER'S JOURNEYS

Meanwhile, the sales organization has developed a sales process. They need to find people who are willing to consider their product or service. They need to inform those people about the features and benefits of their offering. Then they must determine whether the leads they are visiting with are qualified and able to purchase their offering. If we assume that they are professional sellers, they take the time to understand the needs and pain of the customer via a needs assessment or discovery process. Once that pain is found, they present a solution to the customer based on the discovered needs. They will show how the product or service features can provide the benefits that will reduce or eliminate the identified pain. Then they request a commitment to purchase the offering, and they close the sale. For a one-time purchase, this process is complete. Otherwise, there is follow-up and an attempt to develop a deeper relationship after the first purchase using a similar process. We call this "Introduction to Professional Selling" in university sales programs. Both of these processes are shown in figure 6.1.

Figure 6.1. Buyer journey versus sales process.

A key question is whether the buyer's journey and the seller's process align. This question is the center of the sales innovation paradox. They *can* align, but they often do not. When most sales organizations map the customer's journey, they will map their sales process and what they will do for the customer. If the seller connects with the customer with the right message relevant to the buyer's point in their buyer's journey, then the sellers are effective and obtain revenue. But so often, the seller executes a game plan to move their prospects through their marketing funnel, into their sales funnel, and down their pipeline to close. The degree to which that process maps to the individual or segment's journey will determine the frequency and magnitude of success they will obtain for their efforts.

The TABS cycle for the SDR, from the sales organization's perspective, starts with the seller's adjustment to technology by changing their tactics. Sellers have done the following over the past years:

- Increased email contact enabled by automated tools such as sales engagement tools

- Increased phone calls enabled by dialers and assisted dialing

- Increased social media connection and engagement enabled by automation

- Created more videos with tools provided to generate more videos (salesperson-generated video, not marketing)

- Texted customers and potential customers with the aid of sales engagement tools

- Identified customers using data sources to obtain multiple means of message delivery

- Implemented account-based marketing strategies to target key accounts with multithreaded outreach from the selling company to the target firm

The amplified ability of a single salesperson to reach out to their potential market has never been greater. Some would argue that one SDR can now do the outreach or inbound follow-up of 5–10 SDRs from three to five years ago; refer to the math in chapter 2. At the same time, our field has increased the number of SDRs by over 1,200 percent! Let that sink in for just a bit. It doesn't really make much sense, does it? With all this innovation in our field, we should have experienced greater productivity. But we are left with the impression that we have yet to harness our substantial investment in technology and more SDRs fully. But one fact remains: The result is too much noise for the customer.

THE BUYER'S BEHAVIOR SHIFT

Let's consider the impact of all this amplification on the target of this effort, the buyer. Have we had a 1,200 percent increase in the number of buyers? If you consider the Gartner research on the number of people who influence a decision, we might assume that we have 5.8 decision makers.[6] But this research is over five years old, so at best, we have doubled the number of buyers. We have increased the number of people contacting these buyers by over 10 times and have exponentially increased how they can automate the delivery of their outreach. And we have developed strategies for developing sequences and cadence contact points to touch the customer via various channels during our prescribed outreach or follow-up time frame. We have the entire TABS cycle of the seller and the seller organizations summarized. Now, let's move to the new cycle, the sales innovation behavioral shift (SIBS), shown in figure 6.2. How is the customer reacting to the sales innovation or TABS cycle?

- The number of calls it takes to get someone to answer the phone has increased. In 2021, it took 21 calls.[7]

- Click-through rates for emails have dropped off.[8]

- Customers are spending more time researching on their own.[9]

- According to Gartner's work, more buyers prefer a seller-free experience.[10]

- At the same time, they desire more value from salespeople when they need to interact with them.[11]

- Sales effectiveness, as measured by quota attainment, has been below 50 percent for quite some time.[12]

Figure 6.2. SIBS cycle.

In the end, customers are disengaging from the channels used to communicate with them. They are adapting away from the noise we are all creating. But the research shows that they also desire valuable messaging and outreach that addresses their actual needs.[13]

When we consider how goods have been sold throughout history, we can see a pattern of sales innovation or how we communicate value to potential markets via a salesperson. When telephone billing shifted from per-minute charges to a monthly fee, it immediately changed the sales world. Now, salespeople could deliver a message over the phone to any person or business, and we had the birth of telemarketing.

The innovation for the consumer and the businesses was removing per-minute charges for local calls (long-distance rates soon followed). This consumer innovation led to a change in sales motions by salespeople. They could now call both customers and prospects for a monthly fee. Telephone companies were also able to sell lists of phone numbers to companies who wanted to use phones to market and sell their services to businesses or consumers. As more and more companies started calling, the consumer started to dread when the phone would ring. The next innovation was new services for phone lines, including call blocking and caller ID. A behavioral shift occurred here, as people purchased caller ID and the ability to block specific numbers. Caller ID allowed homes and businesses to determine who was calling and to decide whether they should answer. The next move included telemarketing companies using blocked phone numbers, even masked numbers, with no ID. Eventually, consumers demanded the government intervene on their behalf and restrict this behavior. The Telephone Consumer Protection Act (1991) created the National Do Not Call Registry.

From this example, we see the value of a new communication channel, where customers and firms could communicate with each other more efficiently than door-to-door sales. But we also see both the TABS and SIBS cycles as the innovation led to behavioral change and a demand for more technology innovation by both the sellers and the consumers, respectively.

A simple customer economics equation helps us better understand
the SIBS cycle:

Value of the interaction ≥ Cost of the interaction

A prospect, buyer, or customer is willing to interact with a salesperson as long as they perceive that the value they will obtain from this
interaction exceeds the cost. With this equation in mind, when a person
uses a phone to communicate with a friend, relative, or business, we
assume that the value obtained is greater than the cost. However, when
someone calls you commercially, this may not be the case. If the caller
can quickly establish value for the customer, the value exceeds the cost
of being interrupted with a call you didn't expect or want.

We don't only consider the value of the interaction; we develop
the value of the medium—in this case, the phone. The value of the
medium develops on the basis of past experiences with it. If most of
the phone calls we receive are valuable, we value phone calls. However,
when we don't value the interaction, we begin to develop a negative
view of the medium, and we reduce or cease to use it. That's a behavior
shift. Although the example in figure 6.3 is quite dated, it shows the
cycles in action.

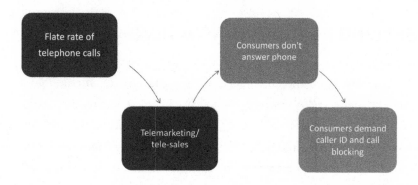

Figure 6.3. SIBS cycle for telemarketing.

It is not that customers, sellers, and businesses don't value using technology to communicate. We still use phones. But the value of receiving messages from that medium is changed when companies or individual sellers use that medium to provide unwanted messaging. Each unwanted message inflicts a cost, and each consumer or business then has a tolerance for that cost. Eventually, the value of a desirable message is too expensive because of the volume of unwanted messaging, and we would expect behavior to shift: The customer stops answering the phone.

We see similar cycles as companies and their salespeople developed commercial use of email. Email has been a highly disruptive force to the postal service, because it drastically reduced the cost of communication between two parties. Its efficiency is apparent. As we see more and more commercial emails, the overall efficiency and value of the medium decreases for consumers and corporate buyers. But the medium is still valued by customers when the messaging is desired and provides value.

We could also go through the social or mobile cycle, but the pattern would be the same: the same use of the medium by sales and the same adjustments by the prospect. Early adopters of these technologies will find success until the customer reaches the behavioral threshold.

SELLING PROCESS INNOVATIONS

Message delivery innovation is not the only area of sales innovation. We have also seen the emergence of new sales process methodologies over the years. *SPIN Selling*, by Neil Rackham, explains the customer's perspective, needs, and pain.[14] Robert Miller and Stephen Heiman developed a methodology for how people make complex decisions.[15] David Sandler developed a set of rules that have grown into a valuable franchise model.[16] In the past decade, we have seen new research and books by CEB (Challenger, Inc.) suggesting that sellers categorized as challengers outperformed other types of sellers during the Great Recession in the late 2000s.[17] Social selling came on the scene in the past decade versus social marketing.[18] And more recently, account-based selling, marketing, and prospecting became new strategies as we closed out the 2010s.

In the recent past, we have seen the rise of inside sales. The change in telecommunications costs has led to a movement that is still growing, moving from field sales forces to inside sales programs. Many, including Anneke Seeley, labeled this movement Sales 2.0.[19] The global COVID-19 pandemic exacerbated this move inside as everyone locked down. Seeley's book provides excellent historical context as she describes the journey to develop the first telephone sales group at Oracle Corporation, called Oracle Direct. She describes the internal challenges to prove the efficiency and efficacy of the model.

Salesforce.com and other SaaS companies were more willing to adopt inside sales teams to develop rapid growth. One lens to see the journey to the first $100 million for Salesforce is captured in Aaron Ross and Marylou Tyler's book *Predictable Revenue*.[20] Many start-ups consider this book the game plan for all companies to reach their first $100 million. At the same time, in the mid-2000s we experienced the Great Recession, which created a perfect opportunity to accelerate the conversion of field sales to inside sales and the rise of the SDR.

During the Great Recession, opportunities were limited, which provided fuel for the movement to inside sales. Companies began to explore the division of labor between pure outreach and actual sales meetings over the phone. This idea led to appointment setters, which then morphed into lead development representatives or SDRs. During this period, the American Association of Inside Sales Professionals expanded into a significant organization that services this community and is now well positioned to influence the sales field. Trish Bertuzzi's book *The Sales Development Playbook* influences many companies' inside sales structures.[21]

The Rise of Social Selling

Social selling can mean many things to many people. Salespeople use social to gather intelligence before meetings or outreach. Sales professionals also use social to listen to prospective and existing clients. Social listening can help sellers gain situational awareness and identify trigger moments when customers may be at a key point in their journey. And of course, social is a platform to connect and communicate. Social media can expand your network or deepen existing social ties with your customer and prospect community, including sending relevant sales messaging.

While social marketing was always available, the growth of LinkedIn as a professional platform had provided a unique place for sellers to engage with professional contacts and prospects. LinkedIn developed the Sales Navigator platform to provide more useful search and communication tools to business-to-business sellers. One of the key advantages of LinkedIn over other social mediums, as we've discussed before, is that its accounts are owned and managed by the professionals themselves. It is doubtful that a gatekeeper, administrator, or social media employee is working on a decision maker's LinkedIn profile. Although it is useful as a cloud-based address book, the fact that we can see and search connections makes the platform very powerful to identify common social relationships and request introductions. Naturally, new training companies were formed to help salespeople in social selling, like Vengresso and Sales for Life. One of the better early books on social selling is from Sales for Life founder Jamie Shanks, *Social Selling Mastery*.[22] A new medium and method of connecting, communicating, and listening to buyers is now available via social media, especially LinkedIn.

Diffusion and Fatigue

Salespeople and organizations develop new methods, models, and processes to sell, whether that is SPIN, Challenger, social selling, account-based marketing, or organizational changes like the birth of the SDR, sales enablement, revenue enablement, and buyer enablement. Once again, it is not the innovation itself that is interesting; it is the degree of adoption of the innovation. The value in this cycle is the adoption from the perspective of the buyer, who experiences the breadth and depth of adoption of a new sales innovation. In this case, the innovation changes the way the seller interacts with the buyer. So understanding the diffusion of the innovation from the buyer's perspective will be the most instructive.

Let's say a salesperson goes to train with Vengresso and learns that using connection requests, the mail feature of LinkedIn, and the InMail feature allow the salesperson one more channel to communicate with existing and potential clients. On the buyer side, they see a connection request. This request's value is assessed on the basis of their view of past connection requests and the relative value of future communications from those connection requests. If past connection requests have been a net positive (employment offers, expertise requests, and valuable networking opportunities), then the buyer would perceive the salesperson's connection request in the light of their past experiences. There is no reason for the buyer to perceive this new opportunity to network differently from past requests. If we assume this happens, each message's arrival allows the buyer to update their view with the arrival of each new connection request.

As more and more salespeople and organizations use LinkedIn to connect to them, the more the buyer has opportunities to update their perceived value of connection requests. The buyer can look at the profile and assess who is requesting a connection to categorize it into buckets that represent *salesperson* and *nonsalesperson*. Although each sales interaction may provide a positive experience for the buyer, it doesn't take too many poorly executed connection requests to shift their perspective. Once the buyer crosses the threshold of negative perception, they will begin to devalue subsequent connection requests.

They will start the process of behavioral shift. Many adaptations are possible, including making their profile private, not accepting connections from people that don't have their email, reporting spam, ignoring requests from salespeople, and even reducing their time on the platform.

Although the salesperson adopts the innovation and adapts to new sales motions and methods, the buyer also experiences new interactions and assesses the relative value of the latest sales motion from their perspective. This perception of value may lead to additional buyer behavioral shifts as they either learn to value or avoid those who use the new methods and motions.

An inbound example may help us fully understand this critical element of the sales innovation paradox and its antidote. If I—as a buyer—first request information via email from a company, I would obviously like to know more about the company, and email is my selected method to receive the information. Perhaps the first few messages and content provide me with valuable information. If so, I value the interaction. But two things can now happen. First, the company may continue to provide me with additional information that I may value. I will update my perception of the importance of this communication over time. If the company provides me with more valuable communication, I find this exchange useful. But if the company sends me information that I do not value, I start devaluing the relationship and the mode of communication. At some point, I become fatigued; I do not value the exchanges anymore. As the customer, I may not even open the email from this sender, or—worse—I may ask to be removed from the mailing list.

But wait; there's more. At the same time that one company finds that email is an effective medium, all the other firms adopt this method, with the same pattern. As more and more companies adopt the same method, the customer computes a value based on many different players. Now the consumer is assessing the value of your communication and the overall value of the means of communication as a whole. They might value your email, but, overall, they find the medium a somewhat tedious mechanism to obtain value. So they then develop adaptive strategies to cope with it. They modify their behavior against the very innovation that they have adopted. As we can see, the diffusion of the innovation is not enough; the depth (the number of emails from one company) and breadth (the number of companies sending emails) of the adoption of the innovation are the crucial aspect. In the case of communication mediums, we can see that the overall value a consumer obtains from the medium is aggregated over all the market players.

We are only considering the good actors in this equation. As more people adopt a medium, players begin to explore the edges of appropriate use. Poor use of a sales innovation can be attributed to many different causes, including inadequate training, inexperience, unethical use, or nefarious purposes. But we all pay the price in consumer fatigue. As buyers shift behaviorally, all future sellers are required to identify the shift and adapt accordingly.

The SIBS cycle is key to the sales innovation paradox. When sales organizations develop scalable sales processes and methods, and buyers are shifting their behavior to these tactics, organizations will see less efficacy with these methods the more the buyer adapts. If the customer shifts, but the sales organizations does not adjust, they experience less efficacy of effort. This is especially true as companies develop industry best practices. Just as the organization is scaling the best practice, the customer segments are shifting and adjusting their behavior to counteract the best practice.

The previous two cycles of TABS for buyers and sellers were regarded as somewhat independent processes. But when salespeople adopt a technology or a methodology, the buyer is the recipient of the sellers' adoption of innovations. As sales professionals and organizations adopt new motions and methods, the customer's reaction to those innovations is likely to predict the ultimate value of the interaction and the payoff to the seller or company.

What Can We Learn?

- Best practices in sales can and often do create a reaction by buyers. The more companies use the same practices, the greater the chance the customer will recognize the tactic and make buyer behavioral adjustments.

- A key challenge to the SIBS cycle is that you are not the only sales organization communicating with your market. It is the collective methods and tactics of all salespeople who contact your prospects and customers who stimulate a behavioral shift.

- As each customer determines their value and related costs of salesperson engagement, the more the use of a new method or tactic by the market as a whole increases the likelihood that customers will devalue these actions and behaviorally shift.

CHAPTER 7

STABS: THE FULL CYCLE

I have so far discussed the TABS and SIBS cycles as independent, but they're not. They occur simultaneously. The buyer has two processes active at all times, and the seller has three processes active at all times. The buyer is always adopting new technology innovations and adapting both their behavior shift from that technology adoption (TABS) and their behavior around both technology and sales interactions (SIBS). The seller is always adopting consumer and corporate technology innovations (TABS) and also adopting sales process innovations (SIBS). Sellers likewise have the opportunity to adapt to technology innovations (consumer and corporate), to adapt to sales process innovations, and to adjust to the buyer's behavioral shift. That is a lot of shifting behavior. The final adaptation is critical: If the buyer is shifting behaviorally, sales must adjust to the customer. I call this complex cycle of cycles the *sales and technology adoption with behavior shifts* (STABS) cycle (see figure 7.1). It is the full process of Spirograph circles that help us dissect the sales innovation paradox.

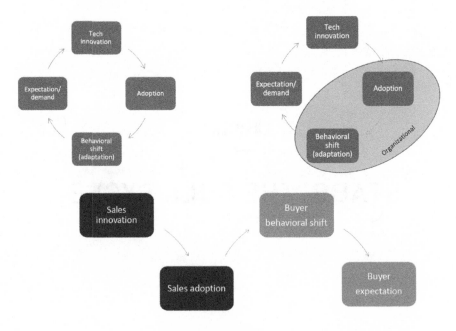

Figure 7.1. STABS cycle.

Sellers and buyers engage in a highly dynamic environment, in continuous motion. Sellers are constantly adapting to technology and sales innovations while also recognizing the adoption and adaptation patterns of the buyers' behavioral shifts. As long as the seller incorporates all of the shifts, their adoption and adaptation will allow them to amplify their efforts and experience productivity gains. So what happens when they miss one or all components of the behavioral shift? When you think about it, this is really quite simple. However, the existing sales methodologies used by most firms may not be adequate for these numerous and complex shifts.

Each TABS cycle starts with a new technology innovation available to the consumer market. This innovation diffuses through the market following models of the diffusion of innovation. Each innovation may have a different diffusion speed, depth of product adoption, and breadth of use. However, not all innovations will create new behavioral patterns in consumers. As more and more people adopt the technology, some adopters begin to develop new habits of use, which often create demand for further innovations. With each new generation of products or services, we see a new diffusion pattern of acceptance and use.

Naturally, buyers and sellers are consumers as well. Just as the buyer begins to shift behaviorally, so do the sellers. It is not uncommon or surprising that market players develop strategies to apply the innovation beyond just the consumer sector once innovation starts its diffusion. We also see a separate diffusion process for businesses and other units, such as governments and nongovernmental organizations.

Sales organization adoption can follow two very different paths. If individual sellers can use the technology independent of the adoption decision of the firm, then we can see a diffusion pattern similar to the consumer sector's. However, when the technology adoption requires firms, teams, or departments to adopt the innovation, the diffusion follows a pattern of discrete jumps at each level. As we discussed earlier, a company's adoption of technology does not necessarily lead to adoption by the individual sellers within that organization. Likewise, as more and more individuals adopt a technology, this does not necessarily lead to organizational adoption. Organizational adoption can also lead to differentiated strategies within sales organizations. This lack of consistent adoption can make it challenging to evaluate the value of the technology at the individual seller, team, or organizational level.

Organizational adoption of an innovation (a technology or sales method) does not have the same diffusion pattern as consumer adoption. Organizational policies and culture may create added friction. Although organizations may have faster diffusion, each organization member will decide whether they will adopt at the individual level. One element of alleviating the sales innovation paradox is to consider this diffusion pattern inside a sales organization.

The second reason this matters is that at any given moment, the prospect firm or client you are working with as a business-to-business seller is experiencing various stages of adoption and adaptation to innovations. Some of those cycles are planned and managed by the leadership. Others are diffusing from the ground up and may not be fully understood or even recognized by the leadership.

When analyzing the seller's cycle, we must move beyond their adoption of technology and consider their adoption rates of new sales methods, processes, and strategies. A new technique or approach may be adopted at the salesperson level, the sales manager lever, the director level, or the sales organization level. However, most methodologies are not fully adopted until they are accepted by the frontline sales managers. They are the ones who can change the actual sales motions of the salespeople. Therefore, sales managers are the key to diffusion of both innovations in technology and process. Sales managers will either facilitate or hinder the organizational adoption of innovation.

Imagine an individual salesperson reads a book, watches a webinar, or goes to training on social selling. They begin to change their sales motions and see some initial results. Since social selling is a multifaceted concept, they begin to understand the breadth of methods with social selling and adopt many different tactics. For example, they don't just look up profiles on LinkedIn before a meeting or a call; they use Sales Navigator to do advanced searches for other decision makers in the firm. Perhaps they even start saving those searches to have a constant stream of new leads based on their search results. As this person adopts a new sales motion—new technology, in this case—the efficiency and effectiveness of their sales efforts amplify, and they start moving up the sales leaderboard at work. The organization did not initiate or manage this adoption, but adoption of the technology has occurred, and the sales innovation paradox is mitigated.

Now let's consider their peers at work or in their social group. As salesperson Mackenzie starts performing well, others start asking what she is doing. Since Mackenzie likes to help her peers, she explains that she has learned about social selling and describes what that means and what she is doing. Soon, her team members start learning about and using social selling. As you might figure, the process then repeats, spreading adoption through the organization.

An opportunity and a risk develop at this point. The frontline sales managers will notice the higher performance and will see the new method's diffusion. Do they create a climate that allows this new method to flourish, or do they hold to existing processes and policy? (Keep in mind that neither approach necessarily changes the individual adoption of the method, especially if it has a better outcome.) Under this level of adoption, the frontline sales manager, director, sales trainer, or sales enablement professional must consider the appropriate action to take. Under the top-down model, the previous example (Mackenzie the social seller) is considered a deviation from the established methodology and the related motions. This sort of top-down, rigid company can stifle effective technology and tactics because of a desire for control.

Even more concerning, what if Mackenzie is a top performer? For example, the company playbook dictates making a certain number of contacts each day—say, 50–100. The sales operations team has determined that salespeople who do this amount of activity each day are more successful. Mackenzie's method develops different motions that may not make it possible to do 50–100 contacts each day, but she may be much more efficient, getting better results than her colleagues who do hit that quota.

Let's say the leadership decides on a social-selling initiative. They introduce the new strategy to their team and implement the plan throughout the organization. In the best cases, frontline sales managers are trained first to reinforce the new sales motions in coaching sessions with their team. Then the salespeople are brought in to learn the latest methods via training of some sort. When the whole organization completes training, this does not mean they have adopted the innovation. Broad-based adoption is more likely since the organization is now fully aware of the innovation, but diffusion is still a decision made by each individual.

The adoption process will most likely be the same as in Mackenzie's case. As individual salespeople experience greater efficiency and effectiveness, they will be more willing to adopt, but the innovation may diffuse faster in the organization than if it was left to the individuals to adopt on their own.

Let's assume that the customer responds positively to the new sales innovation. The sales team will attempt to spread this innovation and scale its delivery. For example, it might be to use a new way to communicate to the customer, like using video messages in cold contacts to make cold outreach via social or email more personal. We will further assume that buyers respond better to this approach, so we get a better response rate.

On the customer side, we have more and more video messaging coming in. With each new video arriving in their email box, social media inbox, and so on, the novelty wears off. Let's isolate a specific ideal customer profile in a highly competitive market—someone on everyone's list. At first, this person finds the idea quite fun and refreshing. It catches their attention and makes the salesperson more genuine and authentic to them. They engage with the video, where they would have just ignored an email, a phone call, or a voicemail. At what point does the novelty of video outreach become less valuable—on the tenth video, the twentieth, the thirtieth? How many videos will it take for the buyer to shift their behavior?

On the sales side, since we see a higher response rate, what are we likely to do? Individual salespeople will adopt, and the organization will attempt to scale. But it's not that simple. Although there are buyers who are seeing this motion for the fiftieth time, other buyers have never received a sales video. The approach is still novel to those who experience it for the first time and to those who only see it once in a while. Likewise, your customers enter a new role in your target segment, and, as you enter segments that have not seen the innovation, the novelty is renewed.

We live in a world where we want to find the best practices and scale those ideas. This thought comes from the Industrial Revolution, in which we sought to mass-produce and systematize our production methods. Such methods work in manufacturing, but they hold less well with business-to-business customers experiencing continual behavior shifts.

A few years ago, I met with a CEO of a SaaS start-up, and he asked me if I had read *Predictable Revenue*.[1] He then told me that it was his game plan. This start-up is now a publicly traded company. How many companies are using this exact game plan? New sales strategies arise each year. We also have the top sales books each year as a source of new ideas. *But we are not manufacturing.* We are not building machines that use resources and create products. We are dealing with human interactions. We are scaling salespeople to use the same techniques and tactics on the same buyers and markets. You cannot outsell your competitors if you use the same tactics, and your customer will never react well to being part of your sales machine.

Perhaps it is time to have an honest discussion about this concept of scaling: what works, to what degree it works, and when it is a waste of resources. Sales is full of opportunities and challenges. If customers were able and willing to buy when they hear about our products and services, there would be a limited need for sales professionals. Sales is helping people bridge the buying gap when the customer cannot buy without assistance. Everything about that concept indicates that sales is not for the weak at heart. But therein lies our problem. Because sales is challenging and requires effort, we are constantly on the hunt for ways to scale a better method or technology. We are always looking to make sales more manageable, more efficient, or more effective.

After World War II, soldiers came home from the war front in the thousands in the United States and around the world. The US economy was focused on a war-based economy, so substantial changes in demand had occurred. Add to this moment that women had entered the workforce in large numbers as men served in the military. So, jobs were scarce at the beginning. Seen from an economist's viewpoint, an excess of labor was available in the marketplace.

Some enterprising companies decided that one way to move more products was to deploy this excess labor door to door to sell products and services to people in their homes rather than waiting for them to come to stores. Imagine being a family living just outside a city. You have to "go to town" to get your needs and wants met. Now imagine your reaction to your first few traveling salesmen. A veteran of World War II comes to your door and offers you products. What a novel idea! You want to support the veteran. You likely find value in the service provided.

From the organizational side, if this is working, what should we do? Scale! This concept is now a best practice. So, your company scales to add more door-to-door salespeople. But wait, there's more. Nothing keeps your competitors from also deploying this new method of generating revenue. Remember, there is an excess of labor available to everyone in the marketplace. But then something odd happens. Door-to-door salespeople start to realize that they now own the relationship with the customer, not the store they work for. So, what's to keep a few enterprising salespeople from going directly to the manufacturer to purchase the products without the local store in the middle? Thus, we get a new source of competition for the stores.

Now, let's think about the poor customer sitting out at the farm. The first few salespeople were novel, helpful, and even made the consumer feel like they were helping employ veterans. At what point do you think they start to dread seeing someone with a suitcase coming up their long driveway with something to sell? In the small communities, cities began making laws to restrict the concept of door-to-door sales to protect their citizens, called Green River Laws.[2]

This exact process occurred with the invention of the telephone. Can you imagine how amazing it must have been to call the local hardware store and order items? You didn't have to go to the store. The ability to call stores to determine whether they had a particular product in stock saved time. At first, phone calls had a cost for each minute of use. So calls were brief and infrequent. Eventually, market forces entered into play, and the price of phone calls decreased. Phone companies needing additional revenue could now sell lists of phone numbers to businesses.

Now, the cost of making a call to a prospective buyer was just the cost of purchasing the list (or just the time to dial randomly until someone answered the phone).

This example is particularly instructive of the complete cycle. Once the cost of calls went down, selling directly to homes and businesses was cheaper for companies. So telemarketing companies were born. There was no barrier to entry, so telemarketing companies could form and develop their products or sell brand-name products faster than the manufacturer could. Buyers moved from answering the phone with excitement to becoming frustrated that the person on the phone was selling them something!

The telephone industry then developed technologies for the home and business to help combat all the telemarketers. Caller ID would indicate who was calling, and voicemail would answer the phone and take a message when you were busy or didn't recognize the phone number. Of course, telecommunications providers also innovated for the telemarketers by offering blocked numbers and new numbers that masked the caller's identity. Eventually, laws prohibited telemarketers from calling people who registered their numbers with the national Do Not Call Registry.

As you can imagine, the whole cycle repeated as, at first, cellphones were expensive and had a per-minute cost. Naturally, more innovation occurred as we moved to mobile phones. In some parts of the world, these mobile phones developed unlimited plans, and telecommunication providers developed ways to provide voice over IP lines that make calls appear to come from specific area codes and regions to mask the identity of the salesperson who is calling.

Thus, we see two examples of the entire cycle of innovation and behavioral change occurring. We could just as easily describe the same cycles for email and social network platforms, or for any future innovation for that matter, because it is a cycle that repeats. We can predict each of the stages of the cycle by looking at the past cycles. Both parties value the innovation at first as a novel way to transact business, with both parties obtaining value from the transaction and the new method of exchanging information. When the innovation reduces the cost of message delivery to the seller's firm, we see an increased use of the innovation by multiple commercial players, including new entrants into the market (resellers) who can scale faster than the incumbent market.

The buyer receives excessive messaging via the innovation channel developed. The cost of this communication then shifts from the seller to the buyer. This shift reduces the value of the innovation to the point of moderated use or disengagement. Citizen consumers will eventually request regulatory action to rectify the consumer costs.

TIMES HAVE CHANGED

The full cycle of sales innovation will repeat itself with each innovation that comes to market. But there is another area of concern: The rate of innovation has accelerated! So we have highlighted our first challenge as sales leaders and business executives.[3]

In the good old days, you could use management concepts to direct market phenomena. You developed the strategy and set the implementation plan to scale innovation and decided on the best practices. More specifically, when a company identified a market shock, it allocated the appropriate time and resources to analyze the change in market conditions. The company adjusted or seized an opportunity by adapting. The company's plans created new strategies and roadmaps to deploy and scale the best practices. Then we spent the time to launch and measure the effectiveness of the plan. Each step in this process took time and resources, but the process was scalable. With appropriate measurements in place, we could identify and deploy best practices across our organizations. Sales leaders could control their methods and innovations, and they could have faith that their efforts would bring about success. We could use management principles from manufacturing in order to scale sales performance and to deploy our sales forces.

What happens if we speed up the cycle? What happens if changes to the environment occur more frequently? When we consider the state of technology innovation in both the consumer and business markets, we are experiencing more consistent shocks to our ecosystem. With frequent shocks, the existing model can be overwhelmed. Our strategies may not be as effective. How does this model hold up if we move from discrete moments of innovation to more continuous innovation cycles?

The model requires time to identify a market change, analyze it, develop a strategy, and deploy that strategy. Given the investments made in training, technology, and strategy, and given the average sales organization's lack of performance improvement, we should question our existing models. Our current strategy is not keeping up in a world where we have moved from a precise moment of innovation to a state of continuous innovation. This is the reason that existing methods are becoming less effective.

While the sales innovation paradox has always existed, what is new about this iteration of the paradox? Velocity has increased to the point that our old models are inefficient for the STABS cycle. It is now more likely that as you change your strategy, the customer and the ecosystem have adjusted to a state different from what your analysis deemed relevant. The continuous STABS cycle requires new strategic capacities from firms, teams, and individual salespeople. Failure to adjust appropriately leads to the sales innovation paradox, but agile and continuous adjustments will create multiplier effects.

THE MULTIPLIER EFFECT

During my first year teaching a graduate sales course at the University of Texas at Dallas, I met a VP of global sales from SoftLayer. Each team of students was to pick a Deloitte's Fast 500 company,[4] interview the sales and marketing executives, and then present how the company had grown so fast. In most years, the slowest three-year growth on that list is just 200 percent or more. The students received a bonus on their assignment if they could get an executive to join their presentation. The sales executive from SoftLayer made the effort to come to class that evening.

SoftLayer had cracked the growth code. During their first few years, they executed a traditional, classic sales machine, go-to-market strategy. They created marketing collateral, hired salespeople, and grew at the same rate as most companies. Then they realized that their buyer had changed. The buyer's needs were agile, but the existing product offerings in cloud hosting were static. So they changed their go-to-market strategy to be designed around the customer's fluctuating needs. Because of the significant growth in application development, start-ups and global companies needed bandwidth to host their apps. But these companies could not predict the need for bandwidth. If the application was broadly adopted and word of mouth spread quickly, they might not have enough, but if they purchased enough bandwidth for a high-growth scenario, their customers might not adopt the application at the same speed, and they would be paying for more than they needed.

So SoftLayer morphed to the market. They offered customers the ability to order bandwidth on demand monthly. They could increase their bandwidth at any time and reduce it as demand fell. They also had to change their cost of acquisition structure to make this work. Customers no longer needed to talk to a salesperson because they wanted to simply order the level of service they required monthly— basically, cloud as a service. They invested more in digital strategies and hired a sales team that focused more on customer guidance than on prospecting and traditional selling.

SoftLayer's earnings grew exponentially. Where they had struggled to get to the first $10 million in revenue, they sailed to over 1,400 percent in growth by having a fully automated digital demand generation model with salespeople who digitally tapped customers stuck in the funnel.[5] When customers had a question or got stuck, the sales team would guide them through their questions and either close the sale or let them order online. The product was responsive to the customer's needs, and the purchasing experience was as simple as requesting a ride from Uber. This whole approach set SoftLayer apart from the other cloud and application hosting markets from a customer viewpoint.

Softlayer realized that they didn't need a sizeable traditional sales force. They were able to scale via digital means and work to increase the efficiency and effectiveness of their sales and marketing funnel. They found that they could grow revenue by tens of millions with no additional sales headcount. Naturally, their compensation model was equally unique. They paid a base salary, but the team also received a portion of the net new revenue generated each quarter in place of an individual commission.[6] Given SoftLayer's impressive growth before the IBM acquisition,[7] their salespeople had some of the highest compensation in the market.

This moment was a game changer for me. I immediately asked the executive to join our advisory board at UT Dallas. Over the years, I would continue to learn from him and the SoftLayer model. But at the same time, I noticed how a vast majority of the market was experiencing stagnant growth and low conversion rates despite their high headcounts—the sales innovation paradox. As I have met with hundreds of companies over the past decade, I have witnessed and helped some of them move beyond the paradox to create a multiplier effect similar to the SoftLayer model.

The SoftLayer story shows that those companies who recognize the sales innovation paradox and develop models, methods, and motions to work within the STABS cycles of their organization and customer will experience multiplier effects.

What Can We Learn?

- Each cycle is not independent. While the sales organization is adapting or scaling, the customer is adopting new technology and adapting to sales innovations; in both cases, they are shifting their behavior.

- Companies that want to be highly effective in this environment will probe and adapt to where the customer is. This means that the salesperson is also adjusting to the customer and buyer behavioral shift.

- Those companies that are able to meet the customer with appropriate adaptation to the behavioral shift will experience substantially better outcomes.

CHAPTER 8

UNDERSTANDING MODERN MOTIONS AND METHODS

The modern seller who understands that modern buyers require modern profiling, frameworks, motions, tools, and skills will often find their efforts are more relevant; this leads to a multiplier effect from their efforts. You can design your sales approach and augment your intelligence with modern motions and tools.

A few years ago, I was briefed on the RASR model (for *results, activities, skills, resources*) by an executive from Xvoyant corporation.[1] For years, many sales executives have found significant traction in the work done by Jason Jordan in *Cracking the Sales Management Code*.[2] A key takeaway from Jordan's book is that managing activities drives results. The RASR model adds that not only do you need to manage activities, but you must also provide resources and develop skills. Because we use a live sales model at UT Dallas, I immediately went to work to adjust our approach to reflect this wisdom.

To provide some clarity and visual context, I would like to introduce a few simple equations to make this chapter more meaningful. A simplification of the Jordan model would be equation (1): As we manage activities, we can then manage results.

Activities → Results   (1)

Jordan's book will help you understand this model and the concept of manageable activities. Xvoyant's RASR model augments the Jordan model by adding that skills and resources compound activities to affect results. This leads to equation (2), with activities as a function of skills and multiplied by resources.

Activities (skills) × Resources = Results   (2)

Before discussing what skills and resources mean, let's introduce the modern methods extension. Equation (3) adds the multiplicative elements of modern motions, which are also a function of modern skills. Stay with me; this is a key moment to understand how to crack the sales innovation paradox.

Activities (skills) × Resources × Motions (skills) = Results × M (3)

When we perform classic activities with modern motions and resources, we experience a multiplier effect (M) on the classic results. This formula for modern results lets us create multiplier effects to end the sales innovation paradox.

ACTIVITIES, SKILLS, RESOURCES, AND MOTIONS

Activities are interactions with our customer or prospect that include outreach touchpoints (email, phone calls, voicemails, etc.), meetings, and other engagements. A key attribute of activities is that they are quantifiably measurable—for example, how many emails, calls, and introductions were completed by a salesperson in a given time frame.

Most of us would agree that just doing an activity is not always sufficient to obtain our objectives; salespeople are required to develop skills related to the activity. These skills are developed by training or by trial and error in the field while practicing on the customer or prospect.

Resources are the tools, collateral, and infrastructure available to assist the seller in serving the buyer. When applied properly and used effectively, resources should have a multiplicative effect rather than an additive one. For example, modern sales tools added to our sales technology stack should increase the efficiency of our activities.

Motions are how activities are performed by sales professionals. A motion describes the adjustment in the activity based on skill, resource allocation, and situation. It is not the action itself; it is the way in which the action is performed. Actions can be performed in a classic or modern way.

To better understand the terms, let's use a sports analogy. In basketball, we witness the activity of dribbling. However, how an individual player dribbles is based on their unique motion. The motion requires skill that develops by training or iteration in the field. We can improve performance by developing skills that allow our sales motions to be effective. This point is valid for both the classic sales machine and modern sales organizations. For simplicity, I propose activities that rely on the classic sales machine motions and related skills and are primarily sales-process driven and most often product-centric. Modern sales motions are primarily driven by the buyer's journey and are customer-centric. Modern motions are evident when the seller uses resources to determine situational relevance and context as they perform a classic method or activity.

MODERN MOTIONS DEFINE MODERN METHODS

Classic motions are based on the classic sales machine (remember CSMI?) and are company- or product-centric. Modern motions are based on the seller understanding the buyer and their journey; they're customer-centric. The activities do not change per se, but the motions that make up the activity are more buyer-centric in a modern context. Being more buyer-centric with our motions will lead to greater sales activity effectiveness, so let's figure out how to modernize our sales motions.

The STABS cycle has behaviorally modified modern buyers. They buy differently because of the impact of technology on their buying and searching activities. Their various interactions in the e-commerce consumer space develop an expectation in the business-to-business buying arena. They expect information to be available on the web and on their mobile phones, and they demand the ability to use social media to gather information from their peers and review sites. They will do a significant amount of research on their own before they contact a salesperson. Gartner reports that 43 percent of customers would prefer not to engage with a salesperson at all.[3]

Not all buyers and situations demand digital paths. Some buyers still find value in engaging with salespeople, at least for certain products. The classic sales concepts of personality styles, state of the company, and status of the individual are all relevant in today's buyer interactions. However, by better understanding a buyer's personality profile and their company's firmographics, the salesperson can better adjust their communication to be more relevant to the situation.

The buyer is also behaviorally modified by the sales interactions they experience. With each salesperson interaction, buyers learn to value, or dislike and avoid, salespeople who use specific techniques or tactics in outreach, meetings, and buyer journey interactions. They are not necessarily reacting to your sales motions and efforts. They are responding to the aggregate actions of the sales profession. Therefore, they are continuously modifying their behavior to both technology and sales innovations (the STABS cycle).

Although it is essential to understand that the customer has changed, it is also vital to realize that organizations have increased the complexity of buying over the past decade. When dealing with more than one buyer, the degree of complexity rises for both the buyer and the seller. The Challenger data first indicated that there were 5.6, then 6.8 decision makers in the average business-to-business buying cycle.[4] Move forward to today, and Gartner and others suggest that this number may be as high as 10.[5] Because buyers expect more digital information, most companies in the business market have answered the call by digitally transforming their businesses. They have developed extensive content about their products and services to address this expectation. There is so much high-quality information that business-to-business influencers and buyers are overwhelmed.[6]

With multiple buyers, sellers must now understand each team member's personality profile, the state of the company and the team, and the status of everyone in the group. With a larger and larger team influencing decisions, the tenure and composition of the buying committee come into play as each deal has a significant risk that influencers may leave or join the company at any time. As churn increases, the risk and complexity of each deal have increased for the seller.

JOBS TO BE DONE

Gartner's sales practice research group has studied the buyer's behavioral migration and the added complexity of larger buying teams and more influencers. They spent time with Clayton Christensen to develop a framework for complex buying[7] based on the jobs to be done by the buyer.[8] The framework indicates that buyers have six jobs to complete before a purchase decision:

- Problem identification

- Solution exploration

- Requirements building

- Supplier selection

- Validation

- Consensus creation

Let's take a few moments to consider what this research is telling us about modern buying journeys. When a buyer is completing a job, this becomes their focal point. They are trying to get that job done. An individual team member performs one job or several at a time. The process is not linear, and according to Gartner, each influencer may revisit each job several times.

This would be complex even if we were talking about only one person, but we are not. We are talking about 10 or more. Now consider that each person who influences the purchase decision may be doing various jobs in their mind. Each snapshot of the company during the buying process is like mapping each individual car during rush-hour traffic to see where each buying team member is at a given point along the journey.

The simplicity of the framework allows us to break down a very complex reality. It also triggers some interesting questions:

- What is the appropriate outreach message to a target company?

- What is the relevant outreach message to an individual buyer?

- What sales methodology is appropriate, given this buying reality (SPIN, Challenger, Sandler, etc.)?

- How can we determine which job the buyer is doing in this framework? How do we map this state for the whole team?

- How should our discovery or needs assessment change, given these states?

- What are the best ways to bring individuals and teams through these jobs so that we can move to purchase?

Buyers and committees are in different stages of the buying journey, so messaging to this reality is critical. When salespeople connect content, outreach, and sales communication to buyer job state, the interaction is more valuable to the customer, and we experience different results. By simplifying the buyer journey into jobs to be completed, we can better address the customer, who provides one of the keys to solving the sales innovation paradox.

A SELLER'S PURPOSE

When companies provide frictionless buying processes using digitally transformed go-to-market strategies, the sales process may look different from the past. Organizations are in danger of using high-cost sales motions to capture revenue rather than more efficient digital channels. If the customer knows their problem, can search for solutions, can develop their own criteria, and can then select their vendor, what is the seller's purpose in the modern buying journey?

Although the buyer's journey is simple to diagram, it's tricky to traverse. With each additional influencer added to the decision, complexity increases, and the risk of losing the sale rises.[9] The buying team has only started this particular journey, but the seller has walked this path with many different customers. They can be an essential guide to the maze ahead. They can help an individual buyer identify the other stakeholders and build consensus at each job that needs to be done.

The client is either aware or unaware of their current problem, and the seller can play a vital role in clarifying it. If the organization is aware of the problem and wants to solve the problem, then a search

for a solution is initiated. Under these conditions, sales or marketing can contact companies with this problem. We call this *inbound
demand generation*.

What if the customers, the market, is not aware? Let's take this on
two levels. First, they are unaware that the product or service you have
developed solves their existing problem. Second, they are not aware
that the problem exists or have misidentified it. Under these conditions, the process will end with a poor purchase or no purchase, or the
buying journey will not even start. When the customer is not aware
of your problem or solution, then marketing may prove insufficient.
These moments provide an opportunity to deploy a sales professional.
A salesperson can help the customer understand both the problem and
their company's solution.

The jobs-to-be-done framework and the customer's state of awareness
lead to both problems and solutions. Leff Bonney has studied the concept of situation awareness in sales.[10] Specifically, he has identified that
a single sales methodology is insufficient for the myriad situations sellers
find buyers in. But going a bit deeper, awareness of the buyer's situation
is helpful in outreach, meetings, and managing the complex buying journey. If a seller can identify the prospect's current state and the different
influencers along their journey, they will be more relevant to the buyer's
current job to be done. Furthermore, if they understand organizational
buying complexity, they will also be aware of the jobs each person influencing the buying decision also has to do.

For years, Robert Miller and Stephen Heiman have helped us categorize the key influencers in a complex buying situation.[11] Understanding
their status, their degree of influence, and whether they win or lose
with each objective is a valuable framework. With the work by Brent
Adamson and others,[12] we can update this language to also consider
that some influencers are more capable of mobilizing the buying team
to a solution than others. With modern technology tools, we can use
AI to identify both the influencers and whether they are mobilizers or
not.[13] With the previously mentioned work by Gartner, we can add the

current job to be done by the buyer or influencer and thereby assess the collective state of the buying team. At this point, the difference between the classic sales machine and modern methods and motions should be coming into focus more.

If the buyer's journey is as complex as is suggested by contemporary research, classic sales processes would appear to be missing the mark, leading to the sales innovation paradox. A properly trained and equipped modern seller would approach each prospect or customer interaction by understanding the aggregate customer journeys that influence an organizational buying team. They would use the resources and develop the skills to help the buyer-influencers complete the jobs that will lead to a buying outcome, as well as recognize those deals and segments that will not lead to a successful outcome.

MODERN TOOLS AND MODERN MOTIONS

So if the context is king in the modern world and situational awareness can foster relevancy, how do we get there? We use modern tools to make modern motions and end the sales innovation paradox. We use personality profile tools from companies like IBM Watson and xiQ to obtain insights on individual prospects to modify our message and approach to their personality, even when we have never met them. We use Sales Navigator to understand the critical company data and identify the potential buyer influencers. We pull a xiQ company dossier to assess its size, funding, and recent social and media footprint.

When salespeople send outreach, we use message tracking tools that communicate with our CRM or sales engagement platform to indicate whether the message has been opened, read, and shared. We use intent data that helps us see customers involved in a buying process or who have our competitor's technology.

When equipped with modern tools, salespeople can be more personalized and relevant in their outreach. Modern sellers will not be so focused on scaling but on probing into the target market with informed messaging. They are in a continuous state of evaluating their effectiveness by using tools that allow A/B testing. They are constantly adapting to the customer shift. They probe for where the customer is in their journey, and they adjust their communications accordingly.

Modern sellers consider the buyer's journey as they plan their subsequent engagement with the customer. They consider the most appropriate purpose for the next engagement: Do they intend to learn or assess, to inform, or to change the state of the customer?

There are many things to learn and assess about buying teams in a complex sale. Who are the influencers of the buying decision?[14] What state do they occupy in the buyer's journey? Do all members of the buying team have the same job to do? What are the communication preferences for each member of the team? Our purpose may be to better understand the prospect rather than the classic motions of just delivering a message.

Once we understand our customers' location along their buyer's journey and understand their preferences, our goal is to help them buy. However, we must know what jobs will need to be done to make this possible. Are our goals to provide information and inform the buyer? Is it to work with their team to complete one of the jobs on the journey to move the team closer to a purchase decision?

Modern sellers do not necessarily follow a set sales process. They use sales methods and skills to assist the customer in completing their buyer's journey by understanding the jobs to be done and by adjusting the purpose of their engagement to help the customer move through those buying tasks. This adjustment makes the seller relevant and valuable to the various members of the buying team.

Let's consider how this would affect prospecting, meetings, and managing a complex deal. If we understood the concepts of behavioral shift, communication preference, personality profiles, and the prospect's current state in their buyer's journey, we would see a different type of outreach. The purpose of cadence and sequencing would not be just to deliver a message but to *find out how to deliver a message.*

When research does not provide adequate insight, early messaging would be more concerned with determining the current buyer's current state rather than delivering a value proposition or a call to action. A modern seller is aware that different levels of effort are appropriate for higher-value opportunities. At the same time, automated methods may be most suitable for smaller deals that are more transactional.

The purpose of a meeting can move beyond assessment, presentation, and closing; it can be to progress the customer in their journey. Although classic sales process motions and methods will be useful, knowing which motions are appropriate at each stage in the buyer's journey to build consensus becomes the driving purpose of meetings. Because complex deals involve multiple influencers, the modern seller is ever aware that there are many reasons that a buying team may need to repeat jobs along the journey. The ongoing assessment of the team's status is essential to being a sense-maker and therefore relevant to the buying team.[15]

WHAT IS THE IMPACT?

Modern sellers who understand the customer's journey in all its dimensions will find that deploying technology will augment their capacity to sell. They will not be sitting on stuck deals in their pipeline; they will be able to diagnose the real reason for the lack of deal progression. They will better assess which deals in the pipeline are moving forward and which are stuck in a state that makes a purchase more or less uncertain. Since they understand the jobs to be done, they will be relevant in their communication and meetings with their clients. Because they are relevant, they are more effective and valued by those clients and prospects. They do not experience the sales innovation paradox because they understand the modern buyer's journey. They use tools to enhance their ability to make an impact and be relevant. They don't worry about scaling; they worry about how to best use their time to make the most impact for their clients. They are multipliers!

What Can We Learn?

- Modern tools allow sellers to better determine where buyers are in their buying journey and to understand buyer preferences.

- Modern sellers who adjust their sales motions to the needs and situation of their buyer will find greater clarity and efficacy; they will be more effective.

- Individuals, teams, and organizations who develop modern skills will find their use of modern motions and tools will lead to multiplier effects.

CHAPTER 9

CREATING MULTIPLIERS

To end the sales innovation paradox, you'll need to develop methods and motions and the skills to implement them, as well as gain support from your organization. Although existing ecosystem factors create sufficient inertia to cause the sales innovation paradox, let's look first at developing an environment that allows and even supports moving away from the sales machine that produces the paradox. Individuals can begin the journey but must be allowed to innovate or deviate from the structured methods and motions of the classic sales machine.

Cracking the performance code at the individual level is the most likely and easiest way to experience the multiplier effect. This level of change only requires a manager to allow for innovation. The next level, a team, would require support from both team members and a director. Although this is possible, the combined forces of structural inertia and human capital pools will exhibit significant forces against innovation, and most teams will revert to the understandable status quo of the classic sales machine.

The highest level of innovation would be at the organization level. This level would require buy-in from the company's sales support structure (or hybrid sales structures[1]), sales executive team, frontline sales managers, and individual sales contributors. At the company level, leadership must reinforce modern motions and methods to counteract the forces of inertia.

A leader can allow, if not outright support, innovation away from the classic sales machine, which produces the sales innovation paradox. With such support, individual pockets of multipliers can be disruptive to the status quo. When a team member is producing at two, five, or 10 times the team's rate and the organization allows other team members to learn and replicate their skills, motions, and methods, a transformation is possible. The disruptor can infect the team with a higher level of performance.

To develop an environment where multipliers can flourish, we should differentiate between the concepts of allowance and support. Support indicates that the organization has an agile and innovative culture that adjusts to modern shifts of both buyers and sellers. At this point in the book, we have established that this is not the norm. Therefore, support for breaking the status quo is a tall order, so we will start with the concept that executives and managers can at least allow deviation within their structured sales machines.

ACTIVITY AND MOTION

The first place to allow variation is at the activity and motion level. Ever since Jason Jordan's book told us that activities are manageable,[2] most organizations have taught managers to track key performance indicators (KPIs). Honestly, we can't generate business without actions, so we manage inputs (activities) to get the outputs (revenue) just like any other manufacturing process. Right? But what would happen if we quit managing or mandating activities?

The first area to allow innovation is in KPIs related to motions and activities. We have already discussed that management theory may not be as helpful, given the modern shifts and the frequency of innovation. So when managers or leaders allow deviation from the prescribed KPIs of the existing sales machine, they allow for experimentation with new motions and methods.

The tolerated innovator would also need to develop new skills. To create those skills, time and perhaps even training outside the organization may be necessary. Although supporting these deviations may be challenging or prohibited, allowing new skills and resources to creep into the organization requires agile leadership from the management and executive teams.

A few years ago, I gave a keynote about the sales innovation paradox at the Sales 3.0 conference in Las Vegas. After the presentation, a sales leader from a professional sports franchise contacted me. He said he was pleased to see that my presentation backed up their bold strategy to end all sales activities. I quickly indicated that I didn't advocate that. He then went on to tell me that his organization had ended all measurement of activities. This change allowed their whole inside sales team to deviate from the sales machine and KPIs. It might sound like abandonment to those of you who are sold on the sales machine.

Well, let's discuss what they did. This organization let the team know that, although activity was necessary, the type and frequency of contact with their prospects were likely better understood by the individual salespeople working an account. The company allocated a set amount of funds for each account for customer engagement (a signed jersey, a concession allocation, seat upgrades, etc.). They placed the ownership of how to use the incentives with the individual contributors. The salespeople knew they would only be accountable for revenue, not other KPIs.

And it worked: The team became one of the most profitable per seat in the NBA. Their inside sales team is about a third the size of other sales teams. It sounds like they accomplished an organizational multiplier culture.

Critical to this story were the resources provided by the organization.

The inside sales manager asked for permission to break the machine, and the leadership not only allowed but supported the experiment. The sales innovation paradox evaporated with use of modern tools and attention to the buyer's journey; the salespeople were allowed to adjust their motions to address the needs of their modern buyers, and this freedom and the reasoned approach produced a multiplier effect.

Although individuals can begin to disrupt the sales machine, there are limits to what they can accomplish without more significant organizational resources and support. When possible, leadership can progress from allowing modern sales methods that deviate from the traditional sales machine to actually supporting them, creating modern motions, skills, and cultures.

Support at the team level would alter the training, activities, motions, tools, and, most likely, the team's composition. For a manager to support modern methods within an organization that was using traditional go-to-market, scalable strategies, motions, and related activities, the manager would first and foremost need to be allowed to do so by the executive leadership. Given that the organization's training, systems, tools, enablement, collateral, and talent acquisition strategies are aligned differently, the task would be sufficiently challenging. The manager would need to develop their means of training and reinforcing modern methods. They would need to find a way to secure an adequate budget for modern sales tools and expand operations and enablement support to achieve modern motions that break from the corporate script. Not only would they need to develop the infrastructure, but they would also need to develop a climate on their team such that the sellers were willing to develop modern sales skills and motions, leaving behind the organization's activity-driven sales culture. The manager can make sure changes happen, but they would be battling change on two fronts: isolating their team from the top-down culture and recruiting people who are willing to execute modern methods. They would also know that the team is operating in a climate that lacks support from the organization and may even be counter to its overall sales culture.

CREATING MULTIPLIERS   115

Such a manager, if successful, would most likely experience one of two outcomes. They might be provided other opportunities, either internally or externally, if they succeeded. Or they might simply succumb to the inertia from both the sales staff and the organization to revert the status quo.

A few years ago, it was not uncommon to see larger organizations like IBM, GE, Microsoft, and Grainger develop new digital teams or groups to explore new go-to-market strategies. The sales technology software industry supports this trend; such companies often approach a potential client suggesting that they test the latest technology with a portion of the organization. A few years ago, you would usually see presentations at conferences that would show the impact of a specific technology like LinkedIn Sales Navigator and modern motions like social selling given to a small portion of the sales team. After a while, management would measure the technology's effectiveness against the control group. This test provides clear evidence of the exploration of modern methods by larger sales organizations.

What is truly unique is the number of times we can see that these experiments with modern tools and motions show multiplier effects presented at various conferences in the field. In these years of the tech stack explosion, I became interested in the automation and augmentation of our field. I sat through presentation after presentation showing the multiplier effects of these experiments.

HYBRID SALES SYSTEMS

A sales organization's primary purpose is to generate revenue. When we consider the components of a sales organization, the fundamental keys are to build, train, and maintain. We start with hiring a leader who has experience. They create the infrastructure to support a trained sales organization, use modern CRM and sales tech stack tools, add sales talent trained and managed by our preferred sales methodology, and generate revenue from the sales machine. More sophisticated organizations would add enablement and operations, and work to cultivate sales and marketing alignment and a more robust recruiting and training model to develop a higher level of performance. Once the sales organization is built, we support it and increase its efficiency and effectiveness with additional innovations. This is a game plan that everyone can develop and deploy. As Scott Santucci would say, sales is simple; simple is hard.[3] But everything just described can produce either the sales innovation paradox or a multiplier effect.

As Robert Peterson and I studied the field of sales enablement during the formation of the Sales Enablement Society, we came to an interesting observation. Most sales support functions, including sales enablement, sales operations, and sales technology, have the sales organization as their customer. Sales enablement, for example, was focused on improving and enhancing the sales organization. In many cases, that means simply improving the efficiency and effectiveness of the already built sales machine. However, in some instances, sales enablement and strategy were focused on both generating revenue from the customer and using sales to accomplish this objective as part of the overall revenue strategy of the company.

This point helps us understand the challenges and opportunities in transforming sales organizations and developing more efficient and effective revenue-generating strategies. Sales contributors, sales managers, teams, directors, and companies can focus on the buyer's motions. Understanding sales motions is simple and can be taught and scaled. We can build a structure around the sales function and work to create, support, and improve its productivity using general management principles. We know how to build a sales machine.[4]

But on the other end of the machine is a buyer. In business-to-business and organizational markets, that customer is another company, with multiple people who may influence the buying decision. The world of the buyer has been and will continue to change over time. Individuals, teams, and organizations designing their revenue-generating strategy around the customer's needs and behavioral shift will experience different results.

Back at the 2017 AA-ISP Leadership Summit, the keynote speaker described Microsoft's Dublin experience.[5] Once again, a significant organization had decided to stand up a new modern sales team. Previously, Microsoft had used web assets as the primary means to capture revenue for the small and medium business segments of the market in Europe. The Dublin arm of the company developed a modern sales team to augment the customer's digital experience with human interaction. Note that the design point is not the sales organization; it is the customer.

They brought in mostly new sales talent to staff this team. This choice was initially essential, because they needed these sales professionals to be part of the customer experience, and not have the customer be part of their sales process. They trained the salespeople from the moment they joined the team to be part of the customer's journey. They had built tools that would provide a view of the customer's journey and then prompt the salesperson to augment it with human interaction, coached by sales technology. This concept was new and built with all the modern methods and motions. As I mentioned earlier, the effect was eight and 10 times the result of the classic approach in pipeline development and pipeline closed, respectively. This multiplier effect was achieved with modern technology and modern sales motions.

The Microsoft Demand Generation team has multiple centers of excellence around the globe. At the 2019 UT Dallas Sales Leadership Summit, Jen Sieger was interviewed and discussed how their demand-generation model led to a 600 percent increase in performance globally with less than a 1 percent increase in headcount.[6]

The Microsoft story is impressive on several levels. First, they were able to deploy digital transformation and modern sales motions, and they were able to replicate the same experience worldwide. Second, although many organizations have witnessed these results, few have been able to sustain or expand on them as the Microsoft Demand Generation team has done. They have achieved the elusive results of harnessing modern technology to increase the efficiency and effectiveness of their revenue-generating team for several years, and they continue to increase it.

So, what are they doing? It first starts with culture at the company and the organizational level. They are a demand generation team, so their culture is focused on the customer, not necessarily the sales organization or function. The customer is the design point of their methods and motions; they are doing all they can to help the customer buy and to assist the seller in helping the customer buy. Their team is constantly thinking about using their demand response team members as efficiently as possible. They have a culture of continuous improvement and adaptation. Last and quite crucially, they have had continuity of strategy and leadership.

The first key point in cracking the sales innovation paradox is to consider the customer as the design point. Sales professionals understand that the customer takes a journey to purchase a product or a service, and that journey has a lot of different jobs that must be completed. Modern sales professionals can use technology to determine the customer's current state. They are also aware that technology and methods create noise in the market, behaviorally modifying the customer's willingness to engage. Modern sellers can adapt their motions and develop their skills to meet the customer on their journey and provide value along their path. The beauty here is that individuals can achieve results without a team or organizational support.

Leadership can allow deviations from the classic sales machine, or they can explicitly drive their organization to support modern skills, motions, and methods by providing all the necessary resources. But they can't stick to business-to-business as usual; the sales innovation paradox can only be overcome with modern tools and a focus on the customer.

What Can We Learn?

- While organizations can develop modern sales motions and skills, it is more likely that individuals and teams will be able to develop and deploy such strategies.

- Management will find the most success by developing a culture that allows agility and innovation. They permit experimentation and encourage their teams to probe and adjust their strategies.

- Those companies that can scale agility and curiosity will consistently develop multiplier effects.

CHAPTER 10

HUMAN CAPITAL INERTIA

From an organizational standpoint, the most crucial diffusion pattern we want to track is the ability of sales professionals, sales organizations, and companies to drive profitable revenue via organizational agility along the customer's journey. Friction may prevent organizations from adopting innovation, which can constrain their salespeople, teams, and the entire organization. If we can better isolate these sources of inertia, we can develop strategies to remove the friction and create multiplier effects.

We have established that customers and individual salespeople are adapting to continuous innovation. The customer is changing because of technology adoption, business innovation adoption, and sales innovation adoption. As our markets adapt, organizations must also adapt; failure to do so will lead to customer frustration and disappointment, as well as a reduced sales force and a lack of marketing effectiveness. By understanding the structural inertia within this system, we can diagnose the factors that lead to the sales innovation paradox and counteract them to create multiplier effects.

Although human capital affects all areas of business, it is especially relevant to revenue generation and particularly to sales and marketing. The human capital pool also makes up the market for our products and services, including organizational customers. The human capital of the firm—owners, executives, management, and workers—possesses knowledge, experience, skills, and a disposition that determine their value to your company and its related organizations, such as client companies and competitors. That knowledge, experience, and skills allow your company to sustain itself. The disposition, or mindset, of each team member also has an impact on the outcomes of that team. More specifically to our focus, these four aspects affect your organization's ability to adapt to the modern sales ecosystem. When an organization can collectively harness its team members' knowledge, experience, and skills, a culture of adoption and adaptation begins to develop. However, these same positive attributes can cause some key team members to resist transformation and avoid adaptation, which will lead to human capital inertia.

For the most part, when we consider candidates for jobs or assess which team members to put on a new project, we consider their existing experience and skills. In most circumstances, we would consider this experience an asset to accomplishing tasks efficiently. However, that experience might lead to reliance on the status quo; a lack of experience in modern motions and methods can lead experienced sales professionals, sales managers, and sales leaders to avoid adopting modern concepts. How do we make use of multiplier effects if we fail to reward—or even hire—the people who know how to create them?

If we value hiring and team formation skills, we hire people with those skills to lead our sales teams. Salespeople and managers who have developed experience and skills in modern motions may not be deemed to have sufficient experience to be selected for assignments and promotions. The very strength that often allows the sales machine to operate effectively may also be a core source of reversion to the status quo. Those who develop modern methods and motions might also experience a harsh environment if the team, organization, or the overall ecosystem provides sufficient pressure to maintain the classic sales machine status quo. This is primarily when existing experience and skills can be easily assessed and developed with known training, coaching, and onboarding processes. Our existing skills and expertise collectively help build our current knowledge of what works within the organization—accepted methods as well as culture.

For some time, organizations have been operating off the management theories developed during the Industrial Revolution.[1] The value of the classic sales machine is that it can be built, it can be measured, it can be managed, and it can be scaled. It is the default strategy for most firms and teams to generate revenue. The existing human capital pool has the needed experience and skills to generate that revenue, so new companies and teams can reach into that stock of talent and hire people to build, manage, and train for the classic sales machine. After a proof of concept is complete and the best practices are identified, it is time to scale. The process used and the skills needed must be easily teachable so that new sales talent can quickly onboard and develop revenue, and entry-level positions in sales need to allow for simple and relatively short onboarding processes. These realities reinforce the classic sales machine and its existing human capital pool.

When a sales professional develops competency and confidence in their ability to generate revenue, to what degree are they willing to try something new? This disposition to adopt new methods and technologies and test new sales motions will determine an organization's capacity to adapt to the preferences of modern buyers. It is not sufficient to simply adopt new technologies. Combining existing sales machine motions and methods with new technology only amplifies the existing strengths or weaknesses. So you might say the adoption of new technologies may produce lower and lower returns—the sales innovation paradox. The willingness of salespeople, managers, leaders, and the enablement team to adapt to the modern seller and then to new technology is critical. However, given the forces involved, these innovators may experience a lack of support when the existing human capital pool is experienced, skilled, and knowledgeable about creating, building, managing, and scaling the classic sales machine.

As you can see, the existing human capital pool is a source of friction that leads to human capital inertia. The distribution of attributes within the human capital pool will directly affect the ability of individuals, teams, and organizations to avoid the sales innovation paradox. A sales professional must have a leader who supports modern methods to experience the potency of combining their activities with modern motions and skills. Conversely, a sales professional with a leader who does not allow deviation from the existing sales machine will likely either become part of the sales innovation paradox or choose to leave the firm.

At the team level, merely having a leader who is conversant and comfortable with modern motions and methods is insufficient to reverse the sales innovation paradox. The leader relies on the attributes of the human capital pool that is willing and able to join their team. If the existing pool has already adopted modern motions and methods, the whole team will create multiplier effects.[2] The next best option would be for the team leader to hire an agile team and be willing to adopt and adapt. However, if the only available talent pool is trained in the classic sales machine, they may be unwilling or unable to adopt and adapt.

When we move to the organizational level, the human capital pool impact looms much larger as a potential source of friction. It is also insufficient for an executive to have adopted and adapted to modern motions and methods. To avoid the sales innovation paradox, the managers and sales professionals who work with that sales executive would need to have already adopted modern methods.

As long as most existing sales managers, trainers, enablement leaders, and executives prefer the status quo, it will be very challenging for them to pull away from it. The sales machine generates revenue, and they have sufficient knowledge and experience about how to scale an organization based on these principles. But maintaining the sales machine has created some precise characteristics and challenges for a firm's revenue.

COMPLEXITY REQUIRES EXPERIENCE

The groundbreaking work by Robert Miller and Stephen Heiman[3] and more recent work by the Challenger researchers[4] have helped identify that sales has been, and continues to become, more complex in the business-to-business sector. More and more influencers are joining the buying process. This level of complexity often leads organizations to require mid-market, enterprise, and government market sales professionals to have experience. Even some small to medium business transactions can move to a complex buying process, which requires years of experience. It is not uncommon to find that companies have taken this experience requirement or preference to the extreme, where most of their sales organization has 20–30 years of experience.

The books *Predictable Revenue*[5] and *The Sales Development Playbook*[6] have influenced many organizations to use manufacturing and economic principles such as the division of labor to develop a modernized sales machine. With more and more complexity and the growth of SaaS purchase models, existing strategies lead the field to consider deploying a division of labor model. This division of labor would create SDRs or lead development representatives primarily responsible for lead generation, inbound communication, and outbound prospecting. In most of these models, the objective is to hand off the qualified prospect once a meeting is scheduled.

The division of labor model has a lot of advantages. It allows the more experienced sellers to spend their time meeting with customers and managing complex sales processes. It should enable account executives to generate more revenue as they are spending their time with customers who are qualified to buy. The SDR/LDR function can use the tedious top-of-funnel process and related sales and marketing activities.

Before this model, a seller would need to understand how to prospect, hold meetings, and manage a complex buying process. Creating new talent or recruiting existing sales talent to accomplish these tasks requires companies to find sales professionals who possess extensive experience and skills to generate revenue. This is very costly, challenging, and time consuming. However, companies can more easily build and maintain sales organizations with the new division of labor model. The company recruits experienced sellers to meet with the customer and manage complex sales processes. Meanwhile, sales leadership develops a new crop of talent that specializes in SDR/LDR work. Given that the prospecting motions are repeatable actions, creating strategies, messaging, training, and managing would be more tractable. As this process has evolved, most organizations have developed onboarding processes that are scalable with entry-level or low-experience talent from the existing human capital pool.

The division of labor model using SDR/LDR and account executives allows the field to address the increasing complexity. Salespeople with existing experience could concentrate more of their efforts on meeting with customers and were no longer required to prospect. However, it is essential to consider the following points.

First, the market's division of labor and the adoption of the SDR/LDR model did not solve the complexity problem. Allowing the SDR to focus on prospecting frees up time for the remaining account executives to focus on meeting with customers and potential customers. However, this division of labor did not directly address the increased complexity identified by Gartner. Subsequent research indicates that most buyers do not find much value from their interaction with salespeople, so more time with clients doesn't necessarily mean that salespeople have developed an understanding of those clients.[7] Although this model may be more efficient, it does not necessarily lead to more effectiveness.

Second, the concept of division of labor assumes that specialization will lead to greater efficiency. I have just questioned the premise that this specialization has led to better outcomes for account executives, but let's address the prospecting side of the labor division. For this strategy to pay off, SDRs would need to stay in their position long enough to understand the product and the assigned segments and to develop the appropriate skills. However, there are two challenges with this assumption. First, most companies and individuals see the SDR role as a stepping stone to the account executive role. Given this context, most SDRs do not intend to stay SDRs. Second, the data indicate that SDRs leave their firms for another SDR position at a frequency that reduces the gains possible from the division of labor. These workers are not in their role long enough to gain the experience and skills to allow the division of labor to create productivity gains.

Finally, the SDR function existing as the training ground for account executives flies in the face of logic. Suppose you divide the labor into two distinct skill sets, prospecting and managing the customer buying process. In that case, it is unclear how prospecting experience leads to the appropriate knowledge and skills needed to manage a complex buying decision. The very fact that the existing sales strategy proposes the functional division for greater efficiency would indicate that ability in one area would not necessarily lead to appropriate skills for the other. Prospectors would develop more transactional skills from repetitive and repeatable activities and sales motions. These skills would not prove helpful in complex buying journeys with multiple decision makers and influencers.

We are seeing trends in our industry that favor the development of two types of salespeople, those who used to manage the whole sales process and those who developed their experience from the new SaaS model. Account executives, the experienced group, would have little to no incentive to understand modern prospecting methods. Their skills to prospect either would atrophy or be irrelevant. And as we have already established, the division of labor did not necessarily address the complexity problem.

Specifically, SDR skills would lean toward short-term objectives (setting a meeting, qualifying a client). Where do the new account executives develop the skills necessary to manage complex buying processes? Would they approach the complex sales process like a transactional sale? This short-term mindset will not address the complexity of constantly shifting behavior, much less undo the sales innovation paradox.

RISK AVERSION AND EXPERIENCE BIAS

Experience bias becomes a significant factor for each group of sellers. The account executives skilled in managing the entire sales process, mentioned above, would be biased toward their experiences of success, including their dated expertise of how to prospect successfully. Meanwhile, the newly trained account executives would have a high probability of having an experience bias toward transactional engagement with clients.

As workers develop skills and knowledge based on their experience, they become confident in their abilities. If this confidence leads to experience bias, all involved have sufficient incentive to develop risk aversion to new methods, motions, and technology. Exploring new motions and technology may require new knowledge and skills. Choosing to adopt and adapt naturally leads to periods of lower confidence and emerging abilities, which may lead to lower outcomes in the short run but with the hope of more significant payoff as these motions are mastered. However, in sales, this is risky. Therefore, it is not surprising that managers, executives, seasoned salespeople, and sometimes even enablement professionals may be overly risk averse to new methods.

When salespeople, managers, executives, trainers, and sales enablement professionals become risk averse and develop experience bias, they significantly contribute to inertia. Their risk aversion may keep them from tolerating the modern sales motions that directly connect with the behavioral shift of modern buyers. Furthermore, when most of the workers in an organization are risk averse and biased, they create greater inertia. In addition, the more companies experience inertia, the more the overall market will experience it.

SALES LEADERSHIP BREEDS HUMAN CAPITAL INERTIA

Sales executives and management can be significant sources of inertia. Most sales managers became managers because of their high level of performance as a salesperson. Likewise, sales executives are often promoted because of their ability to lead a team to a high level of performance as a sales manager. The organization values their knowledge, experience, and skills. This performance-focused talent model produces a performance leadership mindset that usually serves companies well. Effective sales leaders can take their field experience and adapt their knowledge and skills to help their organizations learn from their previous success.

But what happens when that experience and expertise lose their potency because of buyer and seller behavioral shifts? Inertia can set in when sales leaders lean on their past success as the best path forward. This experience bias can lead them to stick with existing strategies, processes, and methods that may lead to the organization failing to adjust to the current reality. Such inertia may cause the organization to fall prey to the sales innovation paradox.

Adopting new methods may erode the competitive advantage of existing management. They may also feel less familiar with and confident in new sales motions and strategies. Leaders who relied on their previous performance for their leadership efficacy will fear both the unknown and the corresponding loss of control that new technology and methods create. We might then see a lack of support for new technology and sales motions from those managers who allow their experience to dictate their view of sales activities and motions. The degree to which they exhibit this performance bias will cause slower change and lead to one more element of human capital inertia.

What Can We Learn?

- Our existing experience bias and promotion preferences lead to human capital inertia, which will inhibit the organization's capacity to crack the sales innovation paradox.

- As buyer decisions become more complex, leaders will have a

greater preference for experienced sales professionals who understand more than appointment setting.

- The current model of sales specialization often fails to create
  economies of scale, which further develops the inertia that feeds
  the sales innovation paradox.

CHAPTER 11

INTERNAL INERTIA

While human capital inertia is about people, those people operate in teams and organizations that face both internal and external environments that create structural inertia, which is most often the root cause of the sales innovation paradox. This inertia is based on the structural realities faced by salespeople, their team, or their organization that may inhibit innovation adoption, including modern sales methods and motions. Let's start with an overview of the internal components of structural inertia.

Internal organizational structures, methods, procedures, policies, cultures, and climates create internal inertia. Existing management experience and theories are the basis of our existing organizational structures. Experience is based on the current team members' past, and the organizational structure and go-to-market strategies are based on those players' combined expertise and knowledge. Experience and known management theory form a team's knowledge. So our current human capital creates our organizational structures, methods, cultures, and climates.

The management principles built for the Industrial Revolution continue to influence our organizational structures. Here, the strategy is often based on a proof of concept followed by the capacity to scale production. As we scale, the idea of specialization or division of labor has led to the development of different departments and roles to allow for production scaling. In production, as we specialize and develop economies of scale, this should lead to higher productivity.

For the revenue-generating part of the business enterprise, we see department structures for sales, marketing, technology, service (customer service or customer success), human resources, and others. Successful companies must have sales and marketing alignment and overall department alignment toward the company's common goal of serving the customer. On the sales side, we see the development of the sales machine that processes the customer from the top of their sales funnel to the purchase. Sales organizations seek the methods and models that will lead to high levels of revenue. The sales machine is designed based on the existing leadership's preferred model.

The recent addition of SDRs allows for job specialization with the goal of greater productivity based on economies of scale. However, SDR roles may only create a new layer of jobs within the existing sales machine. Organizations hire people who understand the components of the sales machine and know how to build and manage the sales machine. This machine requires significant investment and time to develop, and when done correctly, it generates revenue. The inertia between different departments and sales can lead to the sales innovation paradox, and it might develop a culture that fails to support modern methods, motions, and multipliers.

THE KNOWLEDGE OF THE FIRM

Experience and complementary skills provide confidence to help salespeople complete tasks within the sales machine. The collective experience, skills, and knowledge combine to create the firm's human capital pool. The underlying management theories derived from that experience may be causing friction. Let's start with the concept of division of labor.

The Division of Labor Brings Gains

As departments specialize, they develop key performance indicators and other metrics that guide their focus and efforts. The division of labor introduces some natural tension. Each department will develop its priorities and measure its success. One department's success may not be measured by the success of its dependent customer departments. For example, information technology services may value continuity of service as a high priority and may therefore look to standardize their systems. Given what we know about the technology stack explosion in the sales and marketing space, standardization may cause conflict between sales's and marketing's desire to innovate and the ITS department's desire to stay with the standard software they support.

As the degree of dependence between two departments increases, we would expect the alignment between those departments will determine success. The challenge in this case is that division of labor leads the dependent organization, marketing or sales, to not achieve their objectives because of the objectives of the ITS group. This example may not be wholly fair, but it does show a lack of alignment. Although it is true that if sales and marketing don't generate enough revenue, there will be no need for the other departments, such decisions are rarely an existential crisis.

The challenge in this example is relatively straightforward: Sales and marketing would like to add to their technology stack, and this request directly affects the ITS department. If a new technology is purchased, ITS experiences a greater workload and potential conflict with existing systems. Therefore, ITS will experience a cost or a loss. At the same time, the sales or marketing department also experiences the cost of purchasing the software and deploying it to their team. When the purchasing department only assesses their internal department cost and fails to consider the ITS cost, this will lower the return-on-investment threshold of this decision. A lack of alignment toward actual costs will lead to friction against the adoption of new technology.

The Sales and Marketing Alignment Myth

A few years ago, I was convinced that we would see a convergence of marketing and sales. I could see that the digital transformation of the sales field would lead to sales doing marketing and marketing doing sales. I was convinced that this alignment was the key to success. But we must take great care to avoid the sales and marketing alignment myth, which can be another example of interdepartmental inertia.

I am personally a fan of the team at Gartner and the work done by their sales and marketing practice group, including the team that was acquired from CEB a few years back. The research, analysis, reports, and books that have given us the Challenger model,[1] the Challenger Customer,[2] and buyer enablement theories[3] have provided helpful language and concepts to frame our discussion around organizational efficiency and effectiveness. The infamous 5.4 (now 6.8 or more) customers involved in a complex buying decision from their research is an invaluable reality: Sales decisions have become more complex, requiring new sales and marketing approaches to educate, inform, and guide the customer. *The Challenger Customer* moved us beyond the sales organizational structure to the possible buying personas to help develop a strategy for closing complex deals.[4]

Some of the most recent research has been on enhancing the digital assets available to buyers.[5] This research has spawned new language for understanding the customer's buying journey toward a purchase decision. What are the latest sales processes and tactics needed to move organizational influencers to the critical moment of purchase?

From these contemporary trends, language, and frameworks have come a need to align marketing and sales around these new concepts and methods, toward a common goal. In concept, this means that marketing and sales work together cohesively to develop executable strategies and measure the success of new strategies given the ever-changing market needs.

It is not that alignment between sales and marketing isn't crucial; it's that most of the time, the alignment efforts lead to outcomes that make us believe that actual alignment is a myth. Each shift, due to technology, customer behavior, or sales methods, creates an opportunity for sales and marketing to test their degree of alignment.

SOCIAL

The advent of social media has made a considerable impact in the world of marketing. As more and more people connect on social media platforms, marketing departments have yet another means to reach the customer, deliver awareness, and even generate revenue. Marketing departments could develop more significant customer engagement by advertising and creating communities, pages, and groups. Of course, with this innovation came new metrics to consider, like connections, engagements, and so on. Social developed one more channel to add to the firm's marketing and advertising strategy to address diverse segments with content and advertising.

Social not only opened the door for a company to communicate with many people in their social community but also allowed individuals to use social to connect with potential clients, often referred to as *social selling*. Individuals could use social media to communicate with other individuals one at a time or with their network and the world via communities and status updates. What could possibly go wrong here? It sounds like a great moment to align sales and marketing!

The concept of connecting with potential customers on social and using it to communicate with existing customers truly expands the communication capacity of both the company and individual sales-people. However, each social ecosystem has its own rules, which vary as much as individual personalities, expectations, and views of what is appropriate on each platform. But if individual salespeople can use social sites like Twitter and LinkedIn to communicate with their cus-tomers, could they also use social media to meet and broadcast social messages to other customers? If so, who develops the content used by those salespeople and trains them in how to use it? Who owns the rela-tionship if they are using their personal account? Who develops the social-selling strategy—marketing or sales?

A few years ago, many thought leaders preached that every sales-person should become a thought leader and a micromarketer. They should be generating content! Do we really want our salespeople developing creative messaging? Is this the best use of their time? If marketing creates the messaging, will sales use it even when it is clear that it doesn't speak in their voice and from their perspective? Isn't that just social marketing being promoted by employees we ask to share a message? Could this conflict lead to structural or human capi-tal inertia?

It seems highly probable that a social-media-savvy sales leader could attempt to scale their success to their less social-savvy sales organization. Likewise, someone who had a social-selling thought leader as their exec-utive or manager in a previous job might be biased against social selling. This would especially be the case if they had previous experiences where not all their team had success as thought leaders and micromarketers. Each leader creates human capital inertia, which, in turn, may lead to structural inertia. This inertia might be that the sales department is doing the job of marketing, or, in some rare cases, marketing is per-forming sales functions.

Customers do engage with both salespeople and brands on social media. It is also true that this area is rife with challenges that often lead to the sales and marketing alignment myth and both structural and human capital inertia, which leads us to the sales innovation paradox.

VIDEO

Video is the newest opportunity, powerful and expanding. Marketing has used video for many years on television and the internet. YouTube is the second-largest search engine, behind Google (and Google owns YouTube). Recent innovations have allowed us to use video more aggressively, especially on professional social sites like LinkedIn. You can post a video or send a LinkedIn connection a video.

Do we want our salespeople to spend their time developing videos? Would this change who we hire and promote? In a recent trend, influencers have become video famous on LinkedIn, just like on other platforms. So should all our salespeople become the next Daryl (VanillaSoft), Sarah B (Gong.ai), or Shay Longbottom? Is this marketing, or is this sales? Who owns the messaging, the training, and the quality control on social? Should we hire a few influencers to be the face of our brand? What if they leave our brand and work for our competitor? Aren't people their own brand? Do you see the conflict, the alignment myth? It works, but how do we do it? Can you see the sales innovation paradox from the inertia forming within leadership both for and against this use of video?

BEHAVIORAL TARGETING

A few years ago, the *Wall Street Journal* published a series of articles on how much information marketers know about customers.[6] The advent of behavioral targeting allows more efficient allocation of marketing advertising spend to likely buyers. A quick example: You book a flight to Hawaii, but you don't book a car or hotel. As you navigate through your Gmail account, your social media feed, and your favorite news source, you notice that Hawaiian hotels display ads are popping up.

Although these algorithms are well advanced for consumers, will they do the same for companies soon? There is an opportunity for sales and marketing alignment here. This technology could allow companies to identify potential new customers, develop deeper relationships with existing customers, and perhaps even indicate when your current customer is showing signs of defecting to your competition. At the same time, this technology will likely face inertia. If this provides a more efficient ad spend, it might lead to lower allocation for ad dollars. If this innovation allows us to prospect more efficiently, it might lead to less business development headcount. So who will champion this innovation—marketing or sales? Equally likely is the opportunity that the human capital inertia from marketing leaders and sales leaders could lead to this innovation not being explored, let alone adopted. Perhaps this is a moment where sales and marketing align to prohibit the innovation of the firm!

To clarify, the research indicates that sales and marketing alignment is essential and even pays off.[7] Specialization is a fundamental concept of economics. Within a business, there are marketing functions, and there are sales functions. When we talk about marketing from a business-to-business perspective, we are painting a relatively large brush. Marketing is not just customer communications to the target audience; it also includes customer research, product development, branding, and many other functions. So what do we really mean by sales and marketing alignment?

When discussing sales and marketing alignment in the business-to-business market, we usually discuss developing a cohesive go-to-market strategy. To make that strategy cohesive, the collateral and messaging to inform the end customer and the material designed to inform and support the sales organization must all be aligned. The need for these teams to align their efforts, in theory, is indisputable. When this occurs, it can develop a multiplier effect on sales productivity. Although such an outcome is always the goal of most organizations, we more consistently observe the sales alignment myth: Rather than working together for a joint goal, one of the two departments seeks to adjust the other's purpose or strategy or to change their focus. This conflict may lead to realigned resources and organizational influence in the process.

How do we assess an organization's current location on the multiplier versus myth spectrum? As a company services a market, it can show its alignment and agility with each product launch, technology innovation, and behavioral shift. As new product innovations create new opportunities, is the process seamless and revenue-enhancing? Or is it cumbersome and organizationally jarring, with marketing and sales in conflict over segments, product launch timing, pricing, marketing collateral, and sales rollout? Because technology innovation provides the potential for revenue or sales force efficiency, is it a sales-only function managed by a sales-focused sales enablement team? Or does the innovation create a moment of orchestration across departments to develop an effortless experience,[8] to allow a customer to buy products and services from the firm using the most effective coordinated go-to-market strategy?

THE CASE FOR SALES

Given the alignment issue, you might ask, "Do we even need salespeople?" In today's digital environment, most buyers can move from awareness to purchase independently in more and more transactions. Are there situations in which salespeople are simply inefficient at generating revenue? How can your organization best determine this? Can you imagine internal inertia that might cause us never to ask these questions, let alone consider the answers?

The Digital–Sales Buyer Continuum

Let's consider how buyers want to buy. At one end of figure 11.1, we have customers who would prefer to purchase a product digitally without assistance from a salesperson. We see this model pretty consistently in the consumer sector. Customers use digital marketplaces to find, evaluate,

Digital　　　　　　　　　　　　　　　　　　　　　　　Sales

Figure 11.1. The digital–sales buyer continuum.

and purchase the product. The ability to purchase digitally is determined by the nature of the product or service, the company that sells it, and the customer's preference. Small business buyers may tend to act like the consumer market, because a partner or the sole proprietor is making the decision alone. Large companies making a simple purchase or rebuying a product or service are similar. For example, customer segments make simple travel reservations digitally. On the other end of the continuum are those purchases for which assistance from a sales professional is valuable. That value scales with the complexity of the product. The more customizable the product, the more likely the buyer will find value in salesperson interaction to decipher that complexity. Clearly, there is a case for both salespeople and purely digital transactions.

Understanding diffusion and related life cycles of a product or service may allow your company to consider how customers move along the continuum. In most cases, when you introduce a new product, salespeople obtain the initial customers. As familiarity with a product grows for both customers and prospects, these buyers may prefer to move to digital ordering, especially for repeat orders. Forcing a customer to use salespeople in some of these instances may cause unwanted friction in the buying process. As the product matures, customers will be familiar with it, but because of competition in the market, the product may become commoditized. Those who adapt to customers' buying preferences can create a more effortless experience for both the company and the buyer. If they also reduce sales headcount overhead, they can be more reactive on price and customer buying preferences.

However, this is where organizational inertia starts to play a serious role. The market and buyers are moving along a continuum of assistance from high to low need. As we consider the classic sales machine model, there is potential conflict. Just as leadership is scaling to meet demand, the customer no longer wants sales interaction and would prefer a digital exchange. There are many sources of internal conflict and inertia at play at these moments.

The simplest buying process begins when a customer recognizes a need and begins an active search for options to satisfy that need. They develop a set of options and then decide based on that search. In this simple buying model, is there a case for sales? If the customer can achieve these objectives on their own, you could argue that simply providing a digital means of purchasing the product is the best course of action. Among the FAANGM companies, we see clear examples of digital products and transactions without a sales force to guide the customer. When this is possible, it can be highly efficient. Salespeople are costly and may even cause undue friction in the buyer's journey.

The Cost of Friction

Although we want to avoid creating that undue friction, it may also come from other sources. It makes the experience more costly for the customer. If these costs are too high, they may simply not make the purchase and stay with the status quo. This is a significant part of why so many companies' decisions are not making a decision at all.[9]

Jagdish Sheth provides a comprehensive model of industrial buyer behavior (see figure 11.2).[10] One of the first places that can be costly for the customer is gathering decision-critical data and facts. When valuable and accurate information about a product is scarce, the buyer's

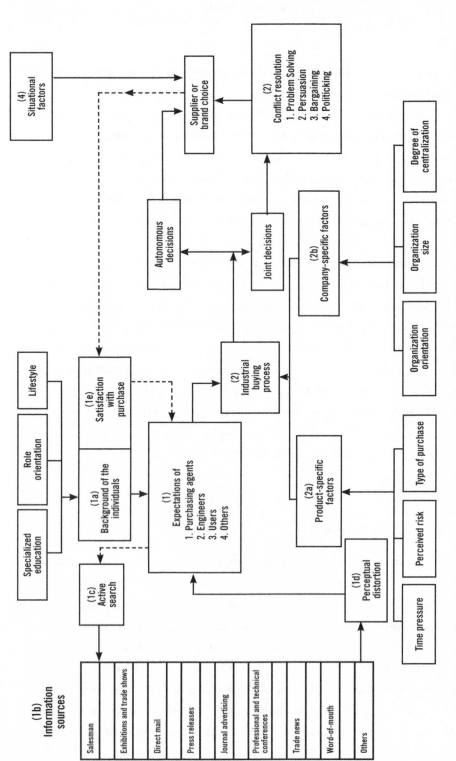

Figure 11.2. Integrative model of industrial buyer behavior. (Source: Jagdish Sheth, "A Model of Industrial Buyer Behavior," *Jagdish Sheth: Thought Leader*, October 1, 1973, https://www.jagsheth.com/consumer-behavior/a-model-of-industrial-buyer-behavior.)

journey is costly. The clarity of each information source can affect the cost of learning about the potential solution.

Once information is gathered and processed, additional friction sources may present themselves in the buying journey. The complexity of the purchase will most likely add to the cost of searching, evaluating, and making a decision. As Sheth indicates, the type of purchase can determine the degree of complexity. When more than one decision maker is involved or when the investment will involve multiple stakeholders, the complexity and friction of the buying process is higher. As we have previously discussed, company factors such as internal inertia can lead to a higher degree of complexity. Complex decisions can be full of friction and, therefore, costly.

Gartner's jobs-to-be-done model indicates that companies can reduce these costs via digital means and sales force deployment, a concept that they have labeled *buyer enablement*.[11] Gartner has determined that customers who purchase in these costly buying situations develop a degree of regret after making the purchase.[12] Buyer enablement helps these customers avoid this regret, which makes them more likely to purchase again.

Active Search

The models by Sheth, Miller and Heiman, Gartner, and Challenger usually start with the idea of active search. In the jobs-to-be-done framework, before a customer completes a purchase, the team must identify the problem to be solved. However, for a buyer's journey to start in earnest, the firm's influencers should experience three essential moments: need arrival, need awareness, and a desire to initiate active search (see figure 11.3).

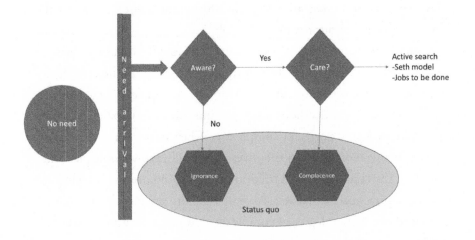

Figure 11.3. Pre-search stages.

As is shown in figure 11.3, without a problem to solve, the buyer has no need. When a problem—and the need to solve it—surfaces, the buyer and the influencers in their organization may still be unaware of it, so they will take no action. Although the customer is unaware of the problem, the firm will experience its consequences. Before the customer's active search can begin, they must recognize the source of those consequences, but this recognition is insufficient. They must also care enough about the problem to take action. Plenty of potential customers are fully aware of their situation and experiencing pain, but are unwilling to begin an active search to solve that problem. The influencers, either individually or collectively, don't care enough. Until someone decides to begin an active search, they will stay in this state.

This is a rich area for experienced salespeople, who can bring value by offering a solution before the customer even knows they need it. They should assess the following:

- Are the stakeholders aware of the problem?

- Is the problem causing sufficient pain for the individual stakeholders and for the organization?

- How complex is the decision, and how much friction is involved?

- Do the key influencers care enough to take action to solve this problem?

Awareness of these critical pre-active-search states provides context for the sales firm to develop better segmentation strategies and fine-tune their ideal customer profiles. Both marketing and sales should consider the effort and the message needed for each segment. An efficient and effective go-to-market strategy would need to consider which segments are worth pursuing and with which tools on the digital sales continuum. Outreach to these pre-active-search states will need to be modified. The firm will need to consider the value of educating the market before the need arrives (most likely via marketing and thought leadership) and of addressing those segments where the condition has arrived. Interaction with salespeople may be more effective than digital messages for customers who are in pain and aware of it. However, the challenge will be maximizing the efficiency of deploying costly sales time and effort. Those customers in active search will likely be our best segment. But in the early stages of their behavioral shift, the lack of awareness may be sufficiently large to warrant a sales-focused go-to-market strategy.

These pre-active-search states provide sufficient motivation to work toward sales and marketing alignment. However, if the organization assumes that all prospects are in the stage of active search, the messaging will not be relevant to the buyer's situation, which causes inertia and the sales innovation paradox.

When a customer can purchase with little friction or complexity, developing a digital path to complete the purchase is the best option. At the same time, deploying salespeople may only add friction to the customer journey and costs to the firm. However, when the process itself creates sufficient friction or when the customer is ignorant of their need, salespeople may be the better investment. If the salesperson can reduce the cost of finding information[13] or can become the most efficient source of information, a sales force may be the best solution. Likewise, when the buying journey becomes overly costly because of complexity, if the salesperson can reduce friction and the costs of navigating the buyer journey, they will provide economic value sufficient to warrant investment in this costly deployment of human capital.

SALES DEPARTMENT INERTIA

Inertia can develop via interdepartmental structures and conflict, but the very structure of the classic sales machine and its modern SaaS extensions are a source of inertia within the sales team.

SaaS

The SaaS sales model provides a particular example of internal inertia in sales. Let's assume the organization deploys a modified sales machine model specialized in meetings and appointment setting. The company has SDRs who prospect and account executives who attend meetings and manage the account growth (some might use customer success for this function). Depending on the organization, the focal point of most SDRs is to get qualified meetings with prospects for their assigned account executives. Companies tie other performance metrics to the number of accounts reached or activities performed. The organization may focus on the ratios of conversion in the funnel. But at the end of the day, the focus is on getting to a meeting with an interested potential customer.

The account executive has a monthly, quarterly, or annual quota. They will need to develop sufficient opportunities in their pipeline to achieve the performance goals indicated by their quota. Although meetings are a vital element of opening opportunities, meetings with potential clients who will choose to purchase within the quota's time frame have to be a priority in order for the account executive to retain their compensation and perhaps even their job.

We have already described that this model is the pervasive current sales machine, especially in the technology SaaS space. The alignment here seems intuitive. But the model is rife with challenges. Each group may focus on potentially divergent goals. One focuses on meetings; the other is focused on closing. Both are reliant on customers who may or may not like the idea of being handed off to another person. As long as the systems remain aligned, we can see progress. However, as with many specializations, when these two functions are not aligned, they may create internal inertia as each group focuses on its own measurement of success.

In this specific case, the dependency is interesting. If the account executive is reliant on the SDRs and the SDRs are not providing sufficient or qualified appointments, the account executive will have a significant and very personal problem. However, if the account executive decides not to trust the source of appointments from the SDR team and decides to generate their meetings, the firm's effort and investment are wasted. This is another example of the critical need to align the various specialized groups to a common objective.

Talent Progression versus the Needs of the Business

From an internal perspective, firms must find a way to balance business needs with their employees' needs and expectations. Conflict and inefficiency arise when the specialized worker does not stay long enough to provide the expected gains from the division of labor. This challenge may be keeping the organization from making serious progress toward modern motions and methods. If the problem is systemic, leadership may seek to simplify those motions and activities because of higher turnover, which would lead to a significant force of internal inertia.

Namely, people don't stay in their positions long enough to develop higher-level skills expected by the modern buyer.

Millennials becoming a significant force in all departments, including and specifically sales, has created a need to adjust strategies to motivate this generation of the human capital pool. One of the adjustments many companies make is to provide frequent and consistent promotions.[14] But how does regular promotion work with the concept of specialization and division of labor? Suppose the customer's needs are more and more demanding and complex, but the salesperson wants to be promoted and move on to new opportunities. How does the firm develop the skills needed and the customer continuity desired? If the customers demand continuity and competence, how does a constantly promoted sales organization provide this?

The quick promotion of millennials is a source of internal inertia. I have witnessed a few strategies to address this conflict. First, the company retains seasoned salespeople to deal with the more complex customers because they do not request or demand constant promotion as their younger counterparts do. Second, they divide the labor into more simplified tasks, the SaaS SDR and account executive model. It is not clear that either of these strategies will allow an organization to address the needs of the complex buyer.

Scale versus Agility

Two additional concepts that create conflict are scale and agility. It is possible to scale and be agile at the same time, but these ideas are also a potential source of internal inertia. When we hire from the human capital pool to build an organization, we often hear this referred to as *scaling*. When a company hires a leader to scale up a sales machine, the leader focuses on the team and resources needed to scale the organization to the desired capacity. You hire the management team members who have scaled successfully in the past. You develop a replicable training and onboarding process. You hire enablement team members to help build the infrastructure around the sales organization. Similarly, you choose and deploy the preferred sales stack of your leadership and enablement team.

How does all this relate to the need to be agile to the behavioral shift of the customer? If the scaling process was agile and adaptive to the customer, it would be a fantastic process to behold. But, typically, when we scale, we need to control the scope of the process we are scaling. We have a set plan and a set go-to-market strategy that needs to get deployed. Therefore, the concept of scaling a sales machine most often does not allow for agility in response to the customer's behavioral shifts. It would be challenging for a leader to support any deviation from the go-to-market machine under construction. Any failures that deviations from the plan might cause would likely receive heightened scrutiny for not following the plan.

So how do we scale but remain agile? It starts with adjusting what we scale. Suppose the purpose of scaling is to build on activities, methods, and strategies for the sales machine. In that case, the two concepts would not conflict if the organization focused onboarding on scaling modern attributes and skills, like agility itself. Teaching sales and marketing teams to do the motions that allowed them to identify and adjust to buyer behavioral shifts would provide modern human capital that would naturally be agile. Similarly, scaling up the skills of researching context and performing situational analysis would allow an organization to address a changing market. The organization should create a culture of curiosity about the customer's environment and their professional and buying journeys.

The organization would also need to move away from title promotion toward skill achievement. In this way, they would engage their workers and provide a clear career path. Rather than opening new promotions based on title, it would create promotions based on skill competency levels. As a salesperson develops skills, their company provides more responsibility and opportunity. Such a model shifts the focus from obtaining a new title to achieving competency. When these skills are directly related to the customer journey, both the firm and the firm's customers will gain. Although a change to pure skill achievement may not be feasible, integrating skill competency into promotion, not just experience bias, would shift the focus and culture of the firm.

Clearly, we have shown that the division of labor in the field of customer revenue acquisition may not always work because of turnover, customer behavioral shifts, and competing definitions of success of different departments. Using technology and directly measuring the impact on revenue would allow the organization to align. Although the division of labor works as a manufacturing principle, we must use some caution as we deploy the same principles in human-to-human interactions like sales and marketing. Companies can achieve efficiency gains via specialization. But we must also keep a keen eye on effectiveness, not just efficiency.

For example, when a firm decides to automate outbound drip campaigns rather than having salespeople sending the email, efficiency is improved (more done with less effort). Let's say we can reach 10 times the number of customers by automating emails. That would be impressive! However, we will also want to keep track of the conversion ratio to ensure automation is not less effective. This lack of effectiveness can show itself in several ways. The lack of personalization in the initial message or follow-up to responses might reduce the conversion ratio. It is also possible that, with so many new leads, the sales organization is unwilling to follow up on all the new leads. Such resistance could be due to a lack of resources (time to make contact) or not selecting leads that provide the best payoff to the salesperson.

The modern buyer's customer journey is in a constant state of behavioral shift. The key challenge for leadership is to mitigate the likely internal inertia that will exert friction against any motions and methods that do not support the status quo of the sales machine. Is the company focused on the voice of the customer, such that sales, marketing, and customer success work to adjust along with the customer's behavior? Is this done cohesively, or are sales and marketing misaligned? The focus on the customer rather than on department initiatives will make the difference between multiplier effects and exponential growth versus the sales innovation paradox caused by inertia.

What Can We Learn?

- Management theory from the Industrial Revolution and the idea of division of labor may not lead us to modern levels of productivity in sales.

- The degree of alignment between dependent departments (or functions) will directly affect the productivity of those departments.

- As salespeople and managers develop the competency to understand customer journeys and behavioral shifts, buyers and customers will find those professionals to be more valuable to their buying process.

CHAPTER 12

EXTERNAL INERTIA

Alongside human capital inertia and internal inertia, we experience inertia from the ecosystem as a whole, called *external inertia*. This includes the buyer's behavioral shifts, ecosystem dynamics, and the interaction between sources of friction.

BUYER SHIFT

Buyers and sellers both modify their behavior around technology. A pivotal point to consider here is how the adoption and adaptation of these various technologies contribute to the overall ecosystem. Still, they may also add to external inertia. Let's take each point independently.

First, as individuals adopt a new technology, there is often a corresponding behavioral shift as they adapt to the use of the technology. The degree of impact on the ecosystem is directly related to both the rate of technology adoption and the degree of adaptation. As more of the market adopts the technology, the aggregate behavioral shift will affect the overall ecosystem. This impact will be at the buyer level, the seller level, the organizational level, and even the societal level.

Second, the idea that the diffusion of an innovation may cause inertia may seem somewhat counterintuitive. By definition, technology adoption is the opposite of inertia. The key here is to consider the adoption's speed and the degree of diffusion related to the adoption. For example, during the early stages of diffusion, only a small market segment has adopted the technology, and even fewer have experienced the corresponding behavioral shift. If a new motion or method is needed to address this market, it exists only in a small segment of the market. As diffusion accelerates and more and more people adopt and adapt, the required change would be more acute as the market grows. There are two sources of inertia at this point. First, if the new motion and method are not as efficient or effective with legacy buyers, then leadership may conclude that the new method is not worth the investment because of its lack of efficacy. Similarly, at the later stage of the adoption curve, part of the market will respond to the legacy technique until diffusion is complete. Therefore, new segments are forming that create an environment where both the modern and the old technique produce income. If you want an example of this phenomenon, just tweet, "Is cold calling dead?" You will see this inertia at play in the resulting argument.

The buyer's behavioral shift caused by sales innovations is clearer. As more and more sales organizations adopt a strategy, the customer begins to see it and may decide to modify their reaction to it. Remember, the first time a sales professional sends you a personalized video, it is unique, and you may find value in this new (for now) approach. Now, let's say 10 percent of your junk mail is videos. Is it still effective? As organizations discover a new method, they will want to scale it to the whole organization. But by definition, if it is a widespread best practice, all the other sales teams will also adopt it. Because the new sales innovation paid off in the early stages, the company will invest in scaling the new method. But the combined impact of this scaling by all the sales organizations may just cause a structural change in buyer segments that devalues the new technique because of its overuse! The structural inertia here worsens when you consider that leaders who had early success with this technique often move to other companies or develop training companies to scale the new method or best practice that is now ineffective.

ECOSYSTEM DYNAMICS

The buyer's behavioral shift lies within a greater dynamic ecosystem that may be the source of significant external inertia that makes avoiding the sales innovation paradox challenging. While many different elements compose the existing external ecosystem, a few seem worthy of further exploration, including the SaaS-ification of the field, the composition of the field, and the frequentist approach to theory and best-practice formation.

The SaaS-ification of the Sales Field

In 2017, the LinkedIn "State of Sales" report indicated that the field had experienced a 580 percent increase in the number of SDRs in the previous three years.[1] From 2018 to 2021, we have seen an additional 71 percent increase (87 percent at the start of the pandemic shutdown) in the 20 major US markets. When you combine these two growth rates, we have had over a 1,200 percent increase in the number of SDRs over the past six to seven years! While impressive, in some cities, the number of SDRs has more than doubled in the past three years alone: Austin (198 percent), Salt Lake City (173 percent), Los Angeles (137 percent), and Miami (124 percent). In 2018, the percentage of sales professionals in sales development was just under half (49.9 percent). In the first quarter of 2021, that percentage of

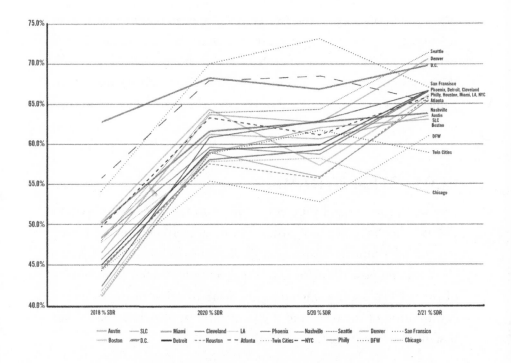

Figure 12.1. Major market changes in SDR from 2018 to 2021.

SDRs was 65 percent, according to LinkedIn data. Figure 12.1 shows the SDR growth from 2018 to 2021 for 20 major markets. The effects of the pandemic are visible, with cities like Chicago, Cleveland, and San Francisco seeing a pronounced drop in SDR share of sales roles. However, it is not clear if this simply represents a migration out of these cities into rural markets.[2]

There is a shift in the sales ecosystem as companies, in aggregate, are moving from hiring and expanding traditional sales roles and investing more in developing talent. One driver of this trend is the expansion of companies in the SaaS space. To illustrate, let's focus on the recent expansion of the marketing and sales tech spaces. From early 2010 to the mid-2010s, we saw an exponential increase in the number of marketing tech companies. Scott Brinker shares that growth has gone from 150 companies in 2011 to 8,000 companies in 2020, as is shown in

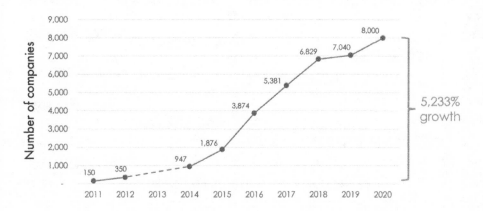

Figure 12.2. Growth of the marketing technology landscape from 2011 to 2020.
(Source: Scott Brinker, "Marketing Technology Landscape Supergraphic (2020): Martech
5000—Really 8,000, but Who's Counting?" *Chief Martec*, April 2020,
https://chiefmartec.com/2020/04/marketing-technology-landscape-2020-martech-5000.)

figure 12.2.[3] Many of these companies have likely hired salespeople, many of which are likely SDRs.

Now let's move over to the sales tech space. In 2021, Sales Hacker reported 1,000 sales technology customers in the market.[4] Nancy Nardin says that the number of companies in her Sales Technology Landscape has grown to over 1,100 (see figure 12.3).[5] We are not here to predict that the sales tech space will match the exponential growth of the marketing tech space. However, these two specialized areas of the SaaS world show us the increase of customers in the SaaS space.

Why is the growth of SaaS leading to the SaaS-ification of the sales field? Let's address a few points. First, business customers are also a key market segment for SaaS sellers. Second, the nature of the SaaS start-up space generates a higher degree of turnover. Third, SaaS-ification is a contributing factor to the SDR explosion and account executive erosion. Fourth, this trend has developed a concept of hiring more SDRs when the efficacy of account executives is dropping off and becoming less profitable.

With the explosion of marketing and sales tech, market segments

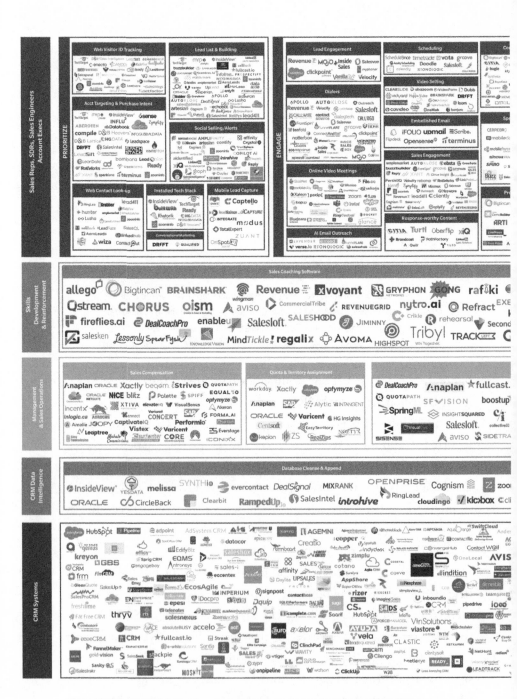

Figure 12.3 Nancy Nardin's enterprise sales tech landscape. (Source: Scott Brinker, "More Evidence That the Golden Age of Salestech Has Arrived," *Chief Martech*, February 2021, https://chiefmartec.com/2021/02/evidence-golden-age-salestech-arrived.)

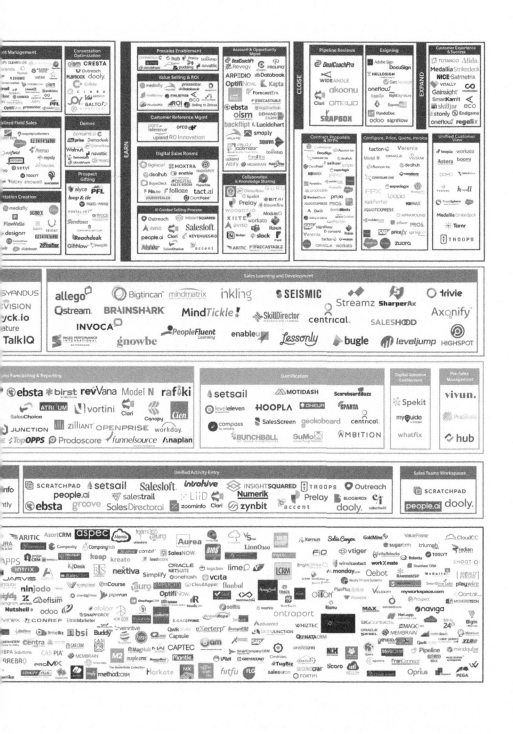

have developed marketing tech for sales technology companies. Although there are many market segments for sales technology, other marketing tech companies provide a market that gets it; selling to this segment would provide quick revenue. So it is possible, and even likely, that the SDRs and, to a degree, account executives learn outreach and value propositioning by selling to their own market. Other SaaS companies will be easier to contact and more likely to understand the innovation and value proposition because they are also trying to approach sales and marketing companies. In this case, the market may be feeding itself. This insular reality would lead to motions and methods that would work well within the marketing tech and SaaS space but would not necessarily transfer to other market segments.

The SaaS start-up space creates a human capital pool that accepts and expects higher turnover and more frequent career transitions. A key source of this turnover culture is venture-capital funding and a lack of financing for companies within this space. At any moment, your company may get new rounds of funding, or if not, they may have to lay off their employees. Funding challenges are not only a force within a company but also an external reality for the human capital pool. With each new round of funding comes a unique opportunity for the market of SDRs and account executives with SaaS sales experience, which further adds to the turnover challenge. We are developing a segment of sales talent that considers low tenure normal.

The SaaS field has been one of the strongest adopters of the SDR/account executive model. SDRs are less costly than account executives and easier to create a talent pool with little to no experience. You might even say that, as account executives drop in efficacy, the favored strategy is to increase the number of SDRs to increase the number of meetings to compensate. This process has developed a massive pool of SDRs but has also removed early-level talent from being trained to be account executives. The LinkedIn data shows almost no growth in sales roles over the past three years, even before the pandemic. In real terms, this may have even been an overall headcount reduction.[6]

The Zs Are Coming

While most organizations have developed their training, promotion, and compensation models for millennials, the coming generation of entry-level talent are not millennials; they are the Z or I generation. Gen Zers are almost orthogonal to millennials, and organizations will soon find that those models will not only disengage Zs but also add to their turnover challenges. Most firms are just experiencing the sources of structural inertia. Companies created recruiting methods, training and onboarding, compensation models, and career paths for the millennial generation. This millennialized model creates experience bias by many managers, directors, and sales enablement professionals. The coming intergenerational conflict is arriving, but most organizations are likely not aware of the root cause, assuming that we are still dealing with other problems related to millennials. All inertia forces will be affected, including human capital and structural forces.

How We Source Talent

Given the lack of sales programs at universities today, let alone 20 years ago, most people don't choose to enter the sales profession. What does this mean for our human capital pool? Most leaders would agree that sales has a relatively low barrier to entry. If the barrier to entry is low, leadership must perceive that anyone could be good in sales. So we develop a war of attrition model at the entry-level side of our field. Many entry-level sales positions, especially in the consumer market, are the survival of the fittest model. If you can fog a mirror, you can get hired, but if you can't perform, you're back on the street.

If this is how we recruit entry-level talent, what about that part of the field that requires experience? Hiring experienced salespeople means we are hiring from the pool that survived the entry-level gauntlet. So our field has a low barrier to entry, which then develops a leadership view that sales talent is easy to hire or create. So how do we pick our leadership?

Although there are many great sales leaders, remember that most obtained their first leadership role by being a top performer. They were promoted so they would not leave. When leaders describe their training process after being promoted, many say they received leadership or management training, but little sales-specific management training.

So if most of our human capital pool of available experienced salespeople, sales managers, and sales leaders come from the survival of the fittest model, does that create internal and external inertia? Some sales executives are more strategic, but over the past 10 years of visiting with leaders who need talent, I have seen that most have developed and come from that survival culture. This executive would tend to model what brought them success when they were a salesperson or a sales manager. However, we have just spent most of this book indicating that consumers and buyers are in a constant state of behavioral shift. The professional journey of most sales professionals and management would most likely serve as a source of both internal and external inertia: Your existing leaders may have experience bias, and the ecosystem perpetuates this challenge.

Theory and Best Practices

After over a decade in sales education, I see most, if not all, departments using backward-looking information to develop forward-looking best practices. Similarly, most theory development is based on frequentist approaches to testing existing and new theories. (A frequentist approach refers to statistical theory, which treats probability in equivalent terms to frequency.) We know that most of the field experiences inertia based on the human capital pool. When we survey the field or the current organization to determine best practices, are we not just capturing what is being done by the majority? The next preferred technique is to compare the top performers with the average or the rest of the organization. What usually follows is a desire to scale the differentiated action of the top performers across the organization.

This method assumes that we should scale what we observe at the highest frequency. It would be helpful as long as it considers technology innovation and buyer behavioral shifts. However, most of the research in this area looks at the sales activities and the outcomes produced by those activities.[7] We then develop theories from these frequentist methods that we use to create our go-to-market strategies. We focus most of this research on sales efforts, so we would likely be biased toward enhancing and building a better classic sales machine. Which is exactly what we see!

When considering what this means to the overall ecosystem, we have sales organizations, researchers, trainers, and enablement professionals looking backward instead of forward. Most organizations increase their headcounts (as shown by the growth in the sales profession) while mechanizing classic sales motions. Based on their preferred motions and messaging, most leadership survived and thrived and therefore looked to perpetuate their own approach. So when we take the time to survey them, we get results that perpetuate the norm and provide inertia.

Combining this across the business-to-business sales ecosystem increases the number of people working within the classic sales machine. We automate and augment their motions based on experience bias. We have increased the number of SDRs by over 1,200 percent over the past few years while at the same time automating their capacity to perform outreach sequences and cold calling touches from 10–100 times what it was. So our capacity to touch the customer has increased by 120–1,200 times. Was there a corresponding increase in the number of buyers over the same time frame? At best estimate, Gartner's research has indicated that buying teams have moved from 6.8 buyers to the mid-teens— twice as many![8] We have found a way to till the buyer landscape over 100 times more than we could just a few years ago.

The sales innovation paradox has led to a Dust Bowl–like sales ecosystem. The buyers are depleted and shifting like the Oklahoma topsoil. Meanwhile, the harvests per acre are dropping. Until we realize that we are ruining the buyer fields with our current methods and motions, our profession will continue to deteriorate.

How These Three Factors Interact

While it is possible to avoid the sales innovation paradox and create multipliers at the individual, team, and organizational levels, sustaining these modern motions and methods will require mitigation of inertia. The external ecosystem, including the available human capital pool, may be a significant force of inertia. Those organizations that build the classic sales machine or develop a survival of the fittest model replenish the human capital pool and sustain internal inertia. This internal inertia and the existing human capital pool aggregate to create an external inertia ecosystem.

These forces will continue as long as most organizations and the human capital pool do not move to modern motions and methods. While we will see pockets of innovation and multiplier effects, we will also continue to see most organizations falling back into the sales innovation paradox. There are decisions to be made by salespeople, managers, executives, sales enablement, and other support services. When I first started this book, it was my view that C-suite leaders needed to move to modern methods and be more efficient and effective with their sales investments. However, it is now more apparent that although commitment by the executive team to move to modern methods would be helpful, it is neither necessary nor sufficient. However, developing a culture that allows sales organizational progression and adjustment to ever-shifting customer behavior is essential. It is sufficient for an individual sales professional to deploy modern methods at the other end of the spectrum. Doing so will cause them to be disruptors of the status quo. Managers, executives, and enablement leaders can either allow or facilitate this deviation from the current sales machine thinking. If they allow the deviation to propagate to other team members and eventually the organization, they might develop a culture that moves from paradox to multipliers. All parties will need to mitigate the natural friction from inertia to reach effective outcomes from their efforts and move the profession into the next era of selling professionalism.

What Can We Learn?

- SaaS-ification of the sales field has changed the skills and competencies of early level talent. It is debatable whether these skills are transferable to other sales roles, especially in complex sales situations.

- The way we source talent, promote to management, and scale creates a self-perpetuating ecosystem that reinforces the sales innovation paradox.

- As executive leadership and management allow and support modern tools, skills, and motions, they will develop pockets of disruption. These pockets will outperform the classic sales machine. Leaders who develop a culture of innovation will experience and grow multiplier effects.

WHAT IS POSSIBLE WITH TODAY'S TECH STACK

Throughout the book, I assert that modern tools will allow you or your company to perform at 10–50 times what was previously possible. While there is evidence of these numbers and many companies have increased their productivity by deploying technology, there is a sufficient number of people who feel that such gains are not tenable. This appendix lays out the gains that are possible with several phases of technology adoption.

A few key points

- Cadence: We will assume a cadence of 20 touches over four different sources (5 touches per source) to obtain an outcome.

- Conversion: Assume one out of 10 prospects convert.

- Effort: Assume 1,000 touches during a time frame, or 50 prospects.

- Results: Baseline assumes five outcomes per time frame.

Phase 1: Clean data sources (+25 percent)

- Assumption: A database that is not constantly updated with clean data sources would have 20 percent incorrect data.

- Technology: LinkedIn, ZoomInfo, SalesIntel, and so on would provide updated data to reduce if not eliminate outreach to bad leads or buyers.

- Control group outcome (four successes): While 1,000 touches are contacted, 200 of the touches were wasted because of bad data.

- Modern group outcome (five successes): All 1,000 touches are viable with clean data.

Phase 2: Communication preferences (+240 percent)

- Assumption: When we identify the prospects' communication preferences, we can reduce the number of touches from 20 to 2.5 on average. How? We will no longer need to use other sources of cadence (saving 15 touches), and their preferred medium will require fewer touches (saving 2.5 touches).

- Technology: LinkedIn Navigator and phone preference services.

- Control group outcome (five successes): 1,000 touches.

- Modern group stage 1 outcome (five successes): 825 touches, 17.5 percent efficiency.

- Modern group stage 2 outcome (12 successes): 1,000 touches, by reinvesting the 175 saved touches into the LinkedIn and phone segments.

Phase 3: Personalization and intent data (+300 percent)

- Assumption: When we use technology to personalize outreach using personality profiles and intent data, we will be able to reduce outreach cadence by two-thirds (only 6.7 touches versus 20).

- Technology: xiQ or IBM Watson and intent data from ZoomInfo.

- Control group outcome: 12 successes, from phase 2.

- Modern group outcome: 36 successes, as we can now contact three times as many people because of greater effectiveness.

Phase 4 and beyond

Additional phases would include developing an ideal customer profile, so that you are contacting people who have a high likelihood of valuing your solution, which would also add to your effectiveness. So far, we have only addressed your effectiveness. Once we have all these things down, we can then deploy technology like assisted dialing (connect and sell) or sales engagement software with AI assistance to increase the effectiveness. With assisted dialing alone, you can increase the number of conversations per time frame by 8–10 times. It is possible to see 10–50 times performance achievement via various methods.

AN EXAMPLE OF MARKET DOMINANCE

In chapter 2, we make a few assumptions:

- Each firm can only hire and train 10 salespeople each month.

- There is a 30 percent turnover rate every six months.

- Each salesperson will obtain 10 customers each month when fully trained.

- Each cohort obtains 15 percent of total capacity each month during training (15 sales each month).

In table B.1, we start with team 1 on the top line. They hire 10 salespeople in the first month. In month two, those salespeople obtain 15 customers (15 percent of capability). In month three, they obtain 30 customers. At the six-month mark, this team is producing 75 sales. In month seven, they would produce 90 sales, but we lose three salespeople because of turnover.

Table B.1 Classic Sales Machine, Inc., ramp (target = 10,000 customers)

Month

	1	2	3	4	5	6	7	8	9	10	11	12
TEAM 1	0	15	30	45	60	75	90	70	70	70	70	70
TEAM 2		0	15	30	45	60	75	90	70	70	70	70
TEAM 3			0	15	30	45	60	75	90	70	70	70
TEAM 4				0	15	30	45	60	75	90	70	70
TEAM 5					0	15	30	45	60	75	90	70
TEAM 6						0	15	30	45	60	75	90
TEAM 7							0	15	30	45	60	75
TEAM 8								0	15	30	45	60
TEAM 9									0	15	30	45
TEAM 10										0	15	30
TEAM 11											0	15
TEAM 12												0
SUM (HIRES)	10	20	30	40	50	50	67	74	81	88	95	99
CUSTOMERS	0	15	45	90	150	225	315	385	455	525	595	665
SUM (CUSTOMERS)	0	15	60	150	300	525	840	1,225	1,680	2,205	2,800	3,465

Each subsequent month, the next team is hired and follows the same sequence as team 1. The bottom three rows show the cumulative hires, customers acquired in that month, and the cumulative customer count. By the end of one year, CSMI will obtain 34.65 percent of the addressable market and have just under 100 salespeople in their organization.

We use similar assumptions for Modern, Inc., with one exception. Modern, Inc., is able to obtain 100 sales per person when fully trained. Given this assumption, they will only need to hire one team of 10 salespeople to address their mark.

As shown in table B.2, we can see the same onboarding gains with 150 sales added each month until month seven. We also see the 30 percent drop-off in month eight caused by turnover. Modern, Inc., is able to capture 66.5 percent of the addressable market by the end of the year. To understand how Modern, Inc., is capable of obtaining 10 times the performance of Classic Sales Machine, Inc., see appendix A.

Table B.2. Modern, Inc., ramp (target = 10,000 customers)

	1	2	3	4	5	6	7	8	9	10	11	12
TEAM 1	0	150	300	450	600	750	900	700	700	700	700	700
SUM (CUSTOMERS)	0	150	450	900	1,500	2,250	3,150	3,850	4,550	5,250	5,950	6,650

NOTES

Foreword

1. Brent Adamson, "Rewriting B2B Selling for Digital Buying," keynote address at the Gartner CSO and Sales Leader Conference, May 17–18, 2021, https://www .linkedin.com/video/live/urn:li:ugcPost:6800072650547834880/.
2. Doug Bushée, "Shift from Seller Enablement to Revenue Enablement," Gartner, 2022, https://www.gartner.com/en/webinars/4014587/ shift-from-seller-enablement-to-revenue-enablement.

Preface

1. Arthur Hughes, *Strategic Database Marketing: The Masterplan for Starting and Managing a Profitable, Customer-Based Marketing Program* (New York: Probus, 1994).
2. Boston Consulting Group, *Perspectives on Experience* (Boston: Boston Consulting Group, 1970).

Introduction

1. CSO Insights, "Fifth Annual Sales Enablement Study," 2019, https:// salesenablement.pro/assets/2019/10/CSO-Insights-5th-Annual-Sales-Enablement -Study.pdf.
2. Robert Peterson and Howard Dover, "Global Perspectives of Sales Enablement: Constituents, Services, and Metrics," *Industrial Marketing Management* 92, no. 1 (2021): 154–162.
3. Deva Rangarajan, Riley Dugan, Maria Rouziou, and Mike Kunkle, "People, Process, and Performance: Setting an Agenda for Sales Enablement Research," *Journal of Personal Selling and Sales Management* 40, no. 3 (2020): 213–220.
4. CSO Insights, "Fifth Annual Sales Enablement Study."

5. LinkedIn, "The State of Sales, 2018," 2018, https://business.linkedin.com/sales-solutions/b2b-sales-strategy-guides/the-state-of-sales-2018.

6. Dover Sales Workforce Project (2022), unpublished data collected by the author to track the trends in sales growth over several years across the 20 major US markets tracked by LinkedIn's Economic Graph.

7. Given the growth in SDR by 1,300 percent and the lack of growth in GDP, the statement is inferred.

8. Steve W. Martin, "The Trend That Is Changing Sales," *Harvard Business Review*, November 4, 2013, https://hbr.org/2013/11/the-trend-that-is-changing-sales.

9. Trish Bertuzzi, *The Sales Development Playbook: Build Repeatable Pipeline and Accelerate Growth with Inside Sales* (Hudson, MA: Moore-Lake, 2016).

10. Aaron Ross and Marylou Tyler, *Predictable Revenue: Turn Your Business into a Sales Machine with the $100 Million Best Practices of Salesforce.com* (Edinburgh, UK: PebbleStorm, 2011).

11. Gartner Research, "Understanding Gartner's Hype Cycles," August 20, 2018, https://www.gartner.com/en/documents/3887767.

12. Gartner Research, "Understanding Gartner's Hype Cycles."

13. Boston Consulting Group, *Perspectives on Experience* (Boston: Boston Consulting Group, 1970).

14. John L. Gustafson, "Moore's Law," in *Encyclopedia of Parallel Computing*, ed. David Padua (Boston, MA: Springer, 2011), https://doi.org/10.1007/978-0-387-09766-4_81.

Chapter 1

1. Hayley Peterson, "More than 9,300 Stores Are Closing in 2019 as the Retail Apocalypse Drags On—Here's the Full List," *Business Insider*, December 23, 2019, https://www.businessinsider.com/stores-closing-in-2019-list-2019-3.

2. McKinsey and Company, "The Quickening," *McKinsey Quarterly* 55 (2020), https://www.mckinsey.com/business-functions/strategy-and-corporate-finance/our-insights/five-fifty-the-quickening.

3. Ethan Smith, "Music Services Overtake CDs for the First Time: Revenue from Downloads Surpass CD Revenue in 2014," *Wall Street Journal*, April 14, 2015, https://www.wsj.com/articles/digital-music-sales-overtake-cds-for-first-time-1429034467.

4. Brad Adgate, "As Media Companies Focus on Streaming, the Audience of Their Cable Networks Continue to Drop," *Forbes*, January 5, 2022, https://www.forbes.com/sites/bradadgate/2022/01/05/as-media-conglomerates-focus-on-streaming-the-audience-of-their-cable-networks-continue-to-drop.

5. Shayndi Raice and Spencer E. Ante, "Insta-Rich: $1 Billion for Instagram," *Wall Street Journal*, April 10, 2012, https://www.wsj.com/articles/SB10001424052702303815404577333840377381670.

6. Reed Albertgotti, Douglas MacMillan, and Evelyn M. Rusli, "Facebook to Pay $19 Billion for WhatsApp," *Wall Street Journal*, February 19, 2014, https://www.wsj .com/articles/facebook-to-buy-whatsapp-for-16-billion-1392847766.

7. Interactive Advertising Bureau, "Covid Ad Spend Impact 2020 and 2021: Light at the End of the Tunnel," September 2, 2020, https://www.iab.com/insights/ covid-ad-spend-impact-2020-2021-light-at-the-end-of-the-tunnel.

8. Scott Brinker, "Marketing Technology Landscape 2022: Search 9,932 Solutions on Martechmap.com," *Chief Martech*, May 2022, https://chiefmartec.com/2022/05/ marketing-technology-landscape-2022-search-9932-solutions-on-martechmap-com.

9. Scott Brinker, "More Evidence That the Golden Age of Salestech Has Arrived," *Chief Martech*, February 2021, https://chiefmartec.com/2021/02/evidence -golden-age-salestech-arrived; Nicolas De Kouchkovsky, "SalesTech Landscape," Cacube Consulting, August 28, 2021, https://www.cacubeconsulting.com/ post/184973176947/salestech-landscape-the-2021-and-7th-edition-of.

10. See the company's website, at https://vendorneutral.com.

11. Pete Wilkins, "G2 Crowd Raises $55M to Transform the Way Businesses Buy Software," *Forbes*, October 11, 2018, https://www.forbes.com/sites/peterandrew wilkins/2018/10/11/g2-crowd-raises-55m-to-transform-the-way-businesses -buy-software.

12. CSO Insights, "Fifth Annual Sales Enablement Study," 2019, https:// salesenablement.pro/assets/2019/10/CSO-Insights-5th-Annual-Sales-Enablement -Study.pdf.

13. LinkedIn, "The State of Sales, 2018," 2018, https://business.linkedin.com/ sales-solutions/b2b-sales-strategy-guides/the-state-of-sales-2018.

14. "What They Know," *WSJ Tech*, accessed June 10, 2022, https://www.wsj.com/news/ types/what-they-know.

15. Robert Peterson and Howard Dover, "Sales Enablement: Definition, Domain, and Future Considerations," *Journal of Selling* 20, no. 1 (2020): 46–59.

16. Robert Peterson and Howard Dover, "Global Perspectives of Sales Enablement: Constituents, Services, and Metrics," *Industrial Marketing Management* 92, no. 1 (2021): 154–162.

17. Peterson and Dover, "Sales Enablement."

Chapter 2

1. Will Bedingfield, "The Race Is On to Stop Scalping Bots from Buying the PS5s," *Wired*, February 2, 2021, https://www.wired.com/story/scalping-bots-buying-all -the-ps5s.

2. Gartner, "Gartner for Sales: 5 Ways the Future of B2B Buying Will Rewrite the Rules of Effective Selling," August 4, 2020, https://emtemp.gcom.cloud/ngw/ globalassets/en/sales-service/documents/trends/5-ways-the-future-of-b2b-buying.pdf.

3. If you would like to see examples of this increase in performance, please refer to appendix A.

4. Dover Sales Workforce Project (2022).

5. Dover Sales Workforce Project (2022).

6. Forrester, "One Million B2B Sales Jobs Eliminated by 2020," April 13, 2015, https://www.forrester.com/press-newsroom/one-million-b2b-sales-jobs-eliminated-by-2020.

7. Matthew Dixon and Brent Adamson, *The Challenger Sale: Taking Control of the Customer Conversation* (London: Penguin, 2011).

8. Gartner, "Gartner Says B2B Sales Organizations Need to Give Customers a Seller-Assisted Digital Buying Experience," May 17, 2021, https://www.gartner.com/en/newsroom/press-releases/gartner-says-b2b-sales-organizations-need-to-give-customers-a-se.

9. Matthew Dixon, Nick Toman, and Rick DeLisi, *The Effortless Experience: Conquering the New Battleground for Customer Loyalty* (New York: Portfolio, 2013).

10. Jordan Bryan, "Sales Must [*sic*] Trusted Resource: B2B Buyers," Gartner, November 5, 2019, https://www.gartner.com/smarterwithgartner/sales-must-trusted-resource-b2b-buyers.

Chapter 3

1. Debbie Dunnam, "Building a World-Class Inside Sales Team from the Ground Up," keynote speech at AA-ISP Leadership Summit, Chicago, April 17, 2017.

2. Jen Sieger, "Microsoft Digital Sales Journey," remarks at UT Dallas Sales Leadership Summit, Dallas, TX, November 5, 2019, https://www.youtube.com/watch?v=WfWD6uJf76o.

3. Robert Seamans and Feng Zhu, "Responses to Entry in Multi-sided Markets: The Impact of Craigslist on Local Newspapers," *Management Science* 60, no. 2 (2014): 476–493.

4. Matthew Dixon and Brent Adamson, *The Challenger Sale: Taking Control of the Customer Conversation* (London: Penguin, 2011).

5. Rachel Louise Ensign, "Bank of America's Merrill Lynch to Ban Trainee Brokers from Making Cold Calls," *Wall Street Journal*, May 24, 2021, https://www.wsj.com/articles/bank-of-americas-merrill-lynch-to-ban-trainee-brokers-from-making-cold-calls-11621850400.

6. Aaron Ross and Marylou Tyler, *Predictable Revenue: Turn Your Business into a Sales Machine with the $100 Million Best Practices of Salesforce.com* (Edinburgh, UK: PebbleStorm, 2011).

7. Trish Bertuzzi, *The Sales Development Playbook: Build Repeatable Pipeline and Accelerate Growth with Inside Sales* (Hudson, MA: Moore-Lake, 2016).

8. Scott Brinker, "More Evidence That the Golden Age of Salestech Has Arrived," *Chief Martec*, February 2021, https://chiefmartec.com/2021/02/evidence-golden-age-salestech-arrived.

9. Nicolas De Kouchkovsky, "All Things Customer Engagement," Cacube Consulting, August 28, 2021, https://www.cacubeconsulting.com/day/2021/08/28; SBI,

"Enterprise SalesTech Landscape," 2022, https://sbigrowth.com/tools-and-solutions/enterprise-salestech-landscape.

10. Laura Silver, "Smartphone Ownership Is Growing Rapidly around the World, but Not Always Equally," Pew Research Center, February 5, 2019, https://www.pew research.org/global/2019/02/05/smartphone-ownership-is-growing-rapidly-around -the-world-but-not-always-equally.

11. Brett Creech, "Are Most Americans Cutting the Cord on Landlines?," US Bureau of Labor Statistics, May 2019, https://www.bls.gov/opub/btn/volume-8/ are-most-americans-cutting-the-cord-on-landlines.htm; Lee Rainie, "Cable and Satellite TV Use Has Dropped Dramatically in the US since 2015," Pew Research Center, March 17, 2021, https://www.pewresearch.org/fact-tank/2021/03/17/ cable-and-satellite-tv-use-has-dropped-dramatically-in-the-u-s-since-2015.

12. Note that SBI purchased Nancy Nardin's IP in 2022; see https://sbigrowth.com/ tools-and-solutions/enterprise-salestech-landscape.

13. "Customers Are More than Just Data: IBM Watson Is Helping Brands See People in the Numbers," *Wired*, February 11, 2016, https://www.wired.co.uk/article/bc/ the-information-revolution-in-commerce.

Chapter 4

1. Everett Rogers, *Diffusion of Innovations*, 5th ed. (New York: Free Press, 2003).

2. Agostino Vollero, Domenico Sardanelli, and Alfonso Siano, "Exploring the Role of the Amazon Effect on Customer Expectations: An Analysis of User Generated Content in Consumer Electronics Retailing," special issue, *Journal of Consumer Behavior* (2022): 1–12, https://onlinelibrary.wiley.com/doi/epdf/10.1002/cb.1969.

3. Tiffani Bova, *Growth IQ: Get Smarter about the Choices That Will Make or Break Your Business* (New York: Portfolio, 2018).

4. Kevin Delaney, "Google in Talks to Buy YouTube for $1.6 Billion," *Wall Street Journal*, October 7, 2006, https://www.wsj.com/articles/SB116014813857884917.

5. Adam Wagner, "Are You Maximizing the Use of Video in Your Content Marketing Strategy?," *Wall Street Journal*, May 15, 2017, https://www.forbes.com/sites/forbes agencycouncil/2017/05/15/are-you-maximizing-the-use-of-video-in-your -content-marketing-strategy.

6. Rupert Neate, "Ryan Kaji, 9, Earns $29.5M as This Year's Highest-Paid YouTuber," *The Guardian*, December 18, 2020, https://www.theguardian.com/technology/2020/ dec/18/ryan-kaji-9-earns-30m-as-this-years-highest-paid-youtuber.

7. Lee Rainie, "Cable and Satellite TV Use Has Dropped Dramatically in the US since 2015," Pew Research Center, March 17, 2021, https://www.pewresearch.org/fact -tank/2021/03/17/cable-and-satellite-tv-use-has-dropped-dramatically-in-the -u-s-since-2015.

Chapter 5

1. Gartner, "Gartner Hype Cycle," accessed July 11, 2022, https://www.gartner.com/en/research/methodologies/gartner-hype-cycle.

2. "Overview: AIDA," *Oxford Reference*, accessed June 10, 2022, https://www.oxfordreference.com/view/10.1093/oi/authority.20110803095432783.

3. Nicolas De Kouchkovsky, "All Things Customer Engagement," Cacube Consulting, August 28, 2021, https://www.cacubeconsulting.com/day/2021/08/28; SBI, "Enterprise SalesTech Landscape," 2022, https://sbigrowth.com/tools-and-solutions/enterprise-salestech-landscape.

4. Wim Biemans, Avinash Malshe, and Jeff S. Johnson, "The Sales-Marketing Interface: A Systematic Literature Review and Directions for Future Research," *Industrial Marketing Management* 102 (April 2022): 324–337.

5. Scott Brinker, "More Evidence That the Golden Age of Salestech Has Arrived," *Chief Martech*, February 2021, https://chiefmartec.com/2021/02/evidence-golden-age-salestech-arrived.

6. De Kouchkovsky, "All Things Customer Engagement."

7. Debbie Dunnam, "Building a World-Class Inside Sales Team from the Ground Up," keynote speech at AA-ISP Leadership Summit, Chicago, April 17, 2017.

8. Jen Sieger, "Microsoft Digital Sales Journey," remarks at UT Dallas Sales Leadership Summit, Dallas, TX, November 5, 2019, https://www.youtube.com/watch?v=WfWD6uJf76o.

9. Dover Sales Workforce Project (2022).

10. XANT, "Sales Development Study, 2021," 2021, https://resources.insidesales.com/wp-content/uploads/2021/03/StateofSalesDev2021.pdf.

Chapter 6

1. Robert B. Miller and Stephen E. Heiman with Tad Tuleja, *The New Strategic Selling: The Unique Sales System Proven Successful by the World's Best Companies* (New York: Grand Central, 2008).

2. Miller, Heiman, and Tuleja, *The New Strategic Selling*.

3. Brent Adamson, Matthew Dixon, Pat Spenner, and Nick Toman, *The Challenger Customer: Selling to the Hidden Influencer Who Can Multiply Your Results* (London: Portfolio, 2015).

4. Allan D. Shocker, Moshe Ben-Akiva, Bruno Boccara, and Prakash Nedungadi, "Consideration Set Influences on Consumer Decision-Making and Choice: Issues, Models and Suggestions," *Marketing Letters* 2, no. 3 (1991): 181–197.

5. Jordan Bryan, "Gartner Keynote: The New Imperative for B2B Sales and Marketing Leaders," Gartner, October 9, 2018, https://www.gartner.com/smarterwithgartner/gartner-keynote-the-new-imperative-for-b2b-sales-and-marketing-leaders.

6. Matthew Dixon and Brent Adamson, *The Challenger Sale: Taking Control of the Customer Conversation* (London: Penguin, 2011).

7. Chris Beal, phone interview by the author, July 12, 2021.

8. Marketing Charts, "Email Click Rates Continue to Decline: Which Emails Perform Better?," November 8, 2019, https://www.marketingcharts.com/digital/email-online-and-mobile-110902.

9. Dixon and Adamson, *The Challenger Sale*.

10. Gartner, "Gartner Says 80% of B2B Sales Interactions between Suppliers and Buyers Will Occur in Digital Channels by 2025," September 15, 2020, https://www.gartner.com/en/newsroom/press-releases/2020-09-15-gartner-says-80--of-b2b-sales-interactions-between-su.

11. Gartner, "Buyer Enablement," accessed June 10, 2022, https://www.gartner.com/en/sales/insights/buyer-enablement.

12. CSO Insights, "Fifth Annual Sales Enablement Study," 2019, https://salesenablement.pro/assets/2019/10/CSO-Insights-5th-Annual-Sales-Enablement-Study.pdf.

13. Gartner, "Buyer Enablement."

14. Neil Rackham, *SPIN Selling: The Best-Validated Sales Method Available Today Developed from Research Studies of 35,000 Sales Calls Used by the Top Sales Forces across the World* (New York: McGraw-Hill, 1988).

15. Miller, Heiman, and Tuleja, *The New Strategic Selling*.

16. David Mattson, *The Sandler Rules: 49 Timeless Selling Principles and How to Apply Them* (Beverly Hills, CA: Pegasus Media World, 2009).

17. Dixon and Adamson, *The Challenger Sale*.

18. Jamie Shanks, *Social Selling Mastery: Scaling Up Your Sales and Marketing Machine for the Digital Buyer* (New York: Wiley, 2016).

19. Anneke Seeley and Brent Holloway, *Sales 2.0: Improve Business Results Using Innovative Sales Practices and Technology* (Hoboken, NJ: Wiley, 2008).

20. Aaron Ross and Marylou Tyler, *Predictable Revenue: Turn Your Business into a Sales Machine with the $100 Million Best Practices of Salesforce.com* (Edinburgh, UK: PebbleStorm, 2011).

21. Trish Bertuzzi, *The Sales Development Playbook: Build Repeatable Pipeline and Accelerate Growth with Inside Sales* (Hudson, MA: Moore-Lake, 2016).

22. Shanks, *Social Selling Mastery*.

Chapter 7

1. Aaron Ross and Marylou Tyler, *Predictable Revenue: Turn Your Business into a Sales Machine with the $100 Million Best Practices of Salesforce.com* (Edinburgh, UK: PebbleStorm, 2011).

2. US Legal, "Green River Ordinance Law and Legal Definition," accessed June 10, 2022, https://definitions.uslegal.com/g/green-river-ordinance.

3. Brian Hopkins, "Why You Are Getting Disrupted," Forrester, May 9, 2017, https://www.forrester.com/blogs/17-05-09-why_you_are_getting_disrupted; Ray Kurzweil,

"The Law of Accelerating Returns," in *Alan Turing: Life and Legacy of a Great Thinker*, ed. Christof Teuscher (Boston, MA: Springer, 2004), 381–416, https://link .springer.com/chapter/10.1007/978-3-662-05642-4_16.

4. Deloitte, "2021 Technology Fast 500 Rankings: The Fastest-Growing Technology and Life Sciences Companies in North America," November 2021, https://www2 .deloitte.com/content/dam/Deloitte/us/Documents/technology-media -telecommunications/us-tmt-fast-500-2021-winners-list.pdf.

5. Deloitte, "Powerful Connections: Deloitte's 2012 Technology Fast 500," 2012, https://www2.deloitte.com/content/dam/Deloitte/us/Documents/technology-media -telecommunications/us-tmt-2012-fast500-winners-brochure-020515.pdf.

6. Various interviews by the author and presentations given by SoftLayer from 2012 to 2015.

7. Spencer Ante, "IBM Pumps Up in Cloud Computing by Buying SoftLayer," *Wall Street Journal*, June 4, 2013, https://www.wsj.com/articles/SB100014241278873245 63004578525001921101148.

Chapter 8

1. Steve Jensen, "RASR Sales Coaching Methodology," Xvoyant, accessed June 10, 2022, https://www.xvoyant.com/resources/the-rasr-coaching-model.

2. Jason Jordan with Michelle Vazzana, *Cracking the Sales Management Code: The Secrets to Measuring and Managing Sales Performance* (New York: McGraw-Hill, 2011).

3. Gartner, "Gartner Says B2B Sales Organizations Need to Give Customers a Seller-Assisted Digital Buying Experience," May 17, 2021, https://www.gartner.com/en/ newsroom/press-releases/gartner-says-b2b-sales-organizations-need-to-give -customers-a-se.

4. Brent Adamson, Matthew Dixon, Pat Spenner, and Nick Toman, *The Challenger Customer: Selling to the Hidden Influencer Who Can Multiply Your Results* (London: Portfolio, 2015).

5. Gartner, "The B2B Buying Journey: The B2B Process Has Changed, Has Your Sales Strategy?," accessed June 10, 2022, https://www.gartner.com/en/sales/insights/ b2b-buying-journey.

6. Gartner, "The B2B Buying Journey."

7. Jordan Bryan, "Gartner Keynote: The New Imperative for B2B Sales and Marketing Leaders," Gartner, October 9, 2018, https://www.gartner.com/smarterwithgartner/ gartner-keynote-the-new-imperative-for-b2b-sales-and-marketing-leaders.

8. Clayton M. Christensen, Taddy Hall, Karen Dillon, and David S. Duncan, *Competing against Luck: The Story of Innovation and Customer Choice* (New York: Harper Business, 2016).

9. Matthew Dixon and Brent Adamson, *The Challenger Sale: Taking Control of the Customer Conversation* (London: Penguin, 2011).

10. Jason Jordan, "New Research from Florida State University Reveals a Critical Flaw in Our Sales Methodologies: An Interview with Leff Bonney, Florida State University

Professor," Sales Education Foundation, November 2019, https://salesfoundation
.org/wp-content/uploads/2019/11/New-Research-FSU-Bonney.2019-Annual.pdf.

11. Robert B. Miller and Stephen E. Heiman with Tad Tuleja, *The New Strategic Selling:
The Unique Sales System Proven Successful by the World's Best Companies* (New York:
Grand Central, 2008).

12. Adamson et al., *The Challenger Customer.*

13. Scott Gillum, "Want to Convert That BSB Sale? You'd Better Be Aware of These 4
Buyer Personalities," *The Drum*, March 22, 2021, https://www.thedrum.com/
opinion/2021/03/22/want-convert-b2b-sale-you-d-better-be-aware-these-4-buyer
-personalities.

14. Miller, Heiman, and Tuleja, *The New Strategic Selling.*

15. David Brock, "Sensemaking: A Framework for Making Sense," *B2C*, March 31,
2019, https://www.business2community.com/strategy/sensemaking-a-framework
-for-making-sense-02207284.

Chapter 9

1. Park Thaichon, Jiraporn Surachartkumtonkun, Sara Quach, Scott Weaven, and
Robert W. Palmatier, "Hybrid Sales Structures in the Age of e-Commerce," *Journal of
Personal Selling and Sales Management* 38, no. 3 (2018): 277–302.

2. Jason Jordan with Michelle Vazzana, *Cracking the Sales Management Code: The Secrets
to Measuring and Managing Sales Performance* (New York: McGraw-Hill, 2011).

3. Scott Santucci, LinkedIn profile, accessed June 10, 2022, https://www.linkedin.com/
in/scottsantucci.

4. Brent Adamson, Matthew Dixon, and Nick Toman, "Dismantling the Sales
Machine," *Harvard Business Review*, November 2013, https://hbr.org/2013/11/
dismantling-the-sales-machine.

5. Debbie Dunnam, "Building a World-Class Inside Sales Team from the Ground Up,"
keynote speech at AA-ISP Leadership Summit, Chicago, April 17, 2017.

6. Jen Sieger, "Microsoft Digital Sales Journey," remarks at the UT Dallas Sales
Leadership Summit, Dallas, TX, November 5, 2019, https://www.youtube.com/
watch?v=WfWD6uJf76o.

Chapter 10

1. Brent Adamson, Matthew Dixon, and Nick Toman, "Dismantling the Sales
Machine," *Harvard Business Review*, November 2013, https://hbr.org/2013/11/
dismantling-the-sales-machine.

2. Tyler Barron (CRO of Encapture), interview by the author, June 2020.

3. Robert B. Miller and Stephen E. Heiman with Tad Tuleja, *The New Strategic Selling:
The Unique Sales System Proven Successful by the World's Best Companies* (New York:
Grand Central, 2008).

4. Brent Adamson, Matthew Dixon, Pat Spenner, and Nick Toman, *The Challenger Customer: Selling to the Hidden Influencer Who Can Multiply Your Results* (London: Portfolio, 2015).

5. Aaron Ross and Marylou Tyler, *Predictable Revenue: Turn Your Business into a Sales Machine with the $100 Million Best Practices of Salesforce.com* (Edinburgh, UK: PebbleStorm, 2011).

6. Trish Bertuzzi, *The Sales Development Playbook: Build Repeatable Pipeline and Accelerate Growth with Inside Sales* (Hudson, MA: Moore-Lake, 2016).

7. Jordan Bryan, "Sales Must [*sic*] Trusted Resource: B2B Buyers," Gartner, November 5, 2019, https://www.gartner.com/smarterwithgartner/sales-must-trusted-resource-b2b-buyers.

Chapter 11

1. Matthew Dixon and Brent Adamson, *The Challenger Sale: Taking Control of the Customer Conversation* (London: Penguin, 2011).

2. Brent Adamson, Matthew Dixon, Pat Spenner, and Nick Toman, *The Challenger Customer: Selling to the Hidden Influencer Who Can Multiply Your Results* (London: Portfolio, 2015).

3. Gartner, "Buyer Enablement," accessed June 10, 2022, https://www.gartner.com/en/sales/insights/buyer-enablement.

4. Adamson et al., *The Challenger Customer*.

5. Jordan Bryan, "Sales Must [*sic*] Trusted Resource: B2B Buyers," Gartner, November 5, 2019, https://www.gartner.com/smarterwithgartner/sales-must-trusted-resource-b2b-buyers.

6. "What They Know," *WSJ Tech*, accessed June 10, 2022, https://www.wsj.com/news/types/what-they-know.

7. Wim Biemans, Avinash Malshe, and Jeff S. Johnson, "The Sales-Marketing Interface: A Systematic Literature Review and Directions for Future Research," *Industrial Marketing Management* 102 (April 2022): 324–337.

8. Matthew Dixon, Nick Toman, and Rick DeLisi, *The Effortless Experience: Conquering the New Battleground for Customer Loyalty* (New York: Portfolio, 2013).

9. Hank Barnes, "94% = Enterprise Buying Teams That Have Abandoned a Buying Effort with No Decision (in the Past 2 Years)," Gartner, September 20, 2016, https://blogs.gartner.com/hank-barnes/2016/09/20/94-enterprise-buying-teams-that-have-abandoned-a-buying-effort-with-no-decision-in-the-past-2-years.

10. Jagdish Sheth, "A Model of Industrial Buyer Behavior," *Jagdish Sheth: Thought Leader*, October 1, 1973, https://www.jagsheth.com/consumer-behavior/a-model-of-industrial-buyer-behavior.

11. Jordan Bryan, "Gartner Keynote: The New Imperative for B2B Sales and Marketing Leaders," Gartner, October 9, 2018, https://www.gartner.com/smarterwithgartner/gartner-keynote-the-new-imperative-for-b2b-sales-and-marketing-leaders.

12. Hank Barnes, "Purchase Regret: The Bane of Land and Expand Strategies," Gartner, September 4, 2018, https://blogs.gartner.com/hank-barnes/2018/09/04/purchase-regret-the-bane-of-land-and-expand-strategies.

13. Sheth, "A Model of Industrial Buyer Behavior."

14. Roy Maurer, "Millennials Expect Raises, Promotions More Often than Older Generations," Society for Human Resource Management, February 26, 2015, https://www.shrm.org/resourcesandtools/hr-topics/talent-acquisition/pages/millennials-raises-promotions-generations.aspx.

Chapter 12

1. LinkedIn, "The State of Sales, 2018," 2018, https://business.linkedin.com/sales-solutions/b2b-sales-strategy-guides/the-state-of-sales-2018.

2. Dover Sales Workforce Project (2022).

3. Scott Brinker, "Marketing Technology Landscape Supergraphic (2020): Martech 5000—Really 8,000, but Who's Counting?," *Chief Martec*, April 2020, https://chiefmartec.com/2020/04/marketing-technology-landscape-2020-martech-5000.

4. Nicolas De Kouchkovsky, "All Things Customer Engagement," Cacube Consulting, August 28, 2021, https://www.cacubeconsulting.com/day/2021/08/28.

5. Scott Brinker, "More Evidence That the Golden Age of Salestech Has Arrived," *Chief Martech*, February 2021, https://chiefmartec.com/2021/02/evidence-golden-age-salestech-arrived.

6. Dover Sales Workforce Project (2022).

7. Jason Jordan with Michelle Vazzana, *Cracking the Sales Management Code: The Secrets to Measuring and Managing Sales Performance* (New York: McGraw-Hill, 2011); Aaron Ross and Marylou Tyler, *Predictable Revenue: Turn Your Business into a Sales Machine with the $100 Million Best Practices of Salesforce.com* (Edinburgh, UK: PebbleStorm, 2011).

8. Gartner, "The B2B Buying Journey: The B2B Process Has Changed, Has Your Sales Strategy?," accessed June 10, 2022, https://www.gartner.com/en/sales/insights/b2b-buying-journey.

ABOUT THE AUTHOR

Dr. Howard Dover is the founder and director of the Center for Professional Sales at the University of Texas at Dallas. Over the past decade, he has trained some of the top entry-level sales producers. Dr. Dover shares his findings and modern methods via various conferences and publications.

He received his bachelor of science in economics from Brigham Young University and his master and doctor of management science from the University of Texas at Dallas. Before his academic life, he founded several companies, including a sales contracting company that he operated for a decade. During his start-up years and government work, he developed the ability to harness technology to increase both the efficiency of business processes and the effectiveness of sales efforts.

Dr. Dover and Amy Dover are the parents of six wonderful children. They currently reside in the Dallas area.

Made in the USA
Coppell, TX
21 January 2024

27984978R00121